A Unique Gamble

A Unique Gamble

Author: Euneke Gammal
Publisher: Euneke Gammal with
Jacqueline R. Turner

A Unique Gamble

Author: Euneke Gammal
Publisher: Euneke Gammal with Jacqueline R. Turner

Library of Congress Control Number: 2020942473

ISBN (paperback): 9781662902871
eISBN: 9781662902888

CONTENTS

FORWARD

The primary purpose of me coming forward with this book, as well as the information therein, isn't, (I Repeat), Is not to expose the people or persons alive or deceased from which I may or may not have sustained the damages outlined. All, of the names have been changed, to protect the innocent, guilty and the indifferent. The Indifferent meaning, those that knew full well all of what was going on but chose to turn a blind eye.

For whatever reason, my primary purpose, past, present, and moving forward, mainly to expose the damaging effects their behaviors and maltreatment has had/still has on me, my loved ones, and their families. To expose this families, generational vicious cycle of abuse, once and for all. More specifically physical, mental, verbal, emotional, psychological abuse. Which have long outlasted my early years of life on planet earth.

In my maturity I have come to realize that there may not be such thing as a perfect family! But there is such a thing as mentally, emotionally, psychologically healthy and sound families. By breaking my silence thereby, exposing the toxicity that lies within, I voluntarily take part, and take a valiant stand with the proactive folk that are: Letting Their Light So Shine! (Matthew 5:15-16) By Telling my truth, that which is true and in full accordance with the facts, as I lived it. Whether folk believe me or not, technically is no longer any of my concern.

CHAPTER 1

My Grandmother Sandra Celeste Gammal lived on Bond St. in a big apartment building that was on the corner, next to the bar. She lived on the 2nd floor. The busiest apartment in the whole building, that was because this family was full of alcoholics. Her place was the place where all her children and their friends would hang out, drink, party and listen to music blaring from the stereo. Her daughter, Hope is one of 4 siblings.

Lived only a few blocks away, toward Broadway in her own apartment with 2 small kids. One named Jackie, who was 5 yrs. old, by the time her little brother Justice was born. Neither child knew their biological fathers, since they both disappeared by the time Hope gave birth. She is now seeing a new fella named Donnie. He is the only one who seemed to show any longterm stability toward her.

They, however, didn't always see eye to eye about everything. Her problem was that she was an alcoholic. Not only that, she enjoyed a good fight while she was drunk! His problem was, he didn't want her to drink, nor be intoxicated around the little ones. This particular night my mother pulled a sneaky move. She bathed the infant, fed him and swaddled him in his blanket, and gently placed him in the middle of the bed where he slept peacefully.

She then snuck out, while Donnie wasn't home, and went up the street to the bar, then came back home, just in time before he arrived. Not knowing he could tell when she had been drinking, she would always become combative as a result, and they ended up fighting.

The argument started in the kitchen, but then quickly escalated into the bedroom. I stood a safe distance away, periodically yelling for them to stop.

As a child watching my mother fight was always a scary time, because I didn't want anyone to get hurt, namely my mother. She'd struck first, and immediately followed up with grabbing a Pabst Blue Ribbon 40oz bottle off the coffee table. Cracked the edge of the table with the bottle, sending shards of glass flying every which way, they squared off, like he was a matador, and she the bull. She came in swinging the jagged edge of what was left of the bottle.

He would jerk his body to either side, this way and that, to avoid being sliced. Backing up slowly while she would step closer and closer to him, until finally he lost his footing and fell backward onto the bed, where my baby brother lay sleeping. She stepped inside his space, they both landed on the bed, she on top, he is trying his best to prevent getting cut by the broken glass bottle.

By holding her wrist, upward & away from his face. as she was coming in with all her might, they both were struggling, and it was a nasty fight indeed. One person trying her best to cut the other person, the other person trying his hardest to prevent being cut, they both were using their brute strength either way. One could hear the grunts of a bull in this fight, at times she would get so close to his face.

He would see it coming in and would push with all his might, this went on for some time, until finally, she overpowered him. In trying to pin his hands down so to get a clean shot at his face, they were right next to the baby. Unbeknownst to her, in pinning his hands down, they landed in the baby's face. Which resulted in slicing the sleeping baby, deeply on his top lip, straight thru to the gum! I screamed no!

Watching it unfold in slow motion, fear ripped through me, I began jumping up and down, I could see the baby was cut, and blood shooting like a geyser from his mouth, each time he breathed out a heart-wrenching scream in pain! There was no doubt about it, all the way to the gumline! Mommy, mommy no! I screamed they were still struggling, never once looking at the screaming baby.

It was only by default that she happened to look at her baby, when Mr. Donnie's head moved in that direction, that she looked up. Otherwise in her blind fury she had not seen, nor heard anything the entire time! Her eyes widened, in shock, and disbelief. Releasing the glass, she leaned over to pick up her, bloody screaming baby! She in a drunken slur, simply said look what you made me do!" scooted off the bed and whisked her bloody crying infant out of the apartment.

Leaving me standing there, Mr. Donnie after he collected himself, left too. So, there I was left alone, eventually, I climbed into the bed and fell asleep. I was a quiet little girl, didn't speak much, except to a very select few of my family members. I often played alone, with my imaginary friends. This was a luxury of mine that allowed me to weave in and out of reality at will, as far as my imaginary limits would carry me.

I was often between homes as a youngster between my mother and grandmother's house all the time. If my mother wanted to go out, she would drop me off at her mother's place, and be off in the wind. While at my grandmothers, she would allow me to play in her hair, scratch her dandruff in her scalp, or rub her feet, digging out any dead skin that she saw which were my favorite things to do.

By the time my mother made her way back to get me, I would scream and cry. Mostly because I'd gotten very comfortable. Besides that, my mother was sort of spooky to me, I was never exactly sure why though, if it was the way she looked at me? As if to say, I'm going to kill you little girl. I just couldn't put my finger on it. This particular day, at home with my mother she made dinner. Potatoes, meat and cooked carrots.

She never allowed me in the kitchen with her while she cooked. I stayed in the front room quietly entertaining myself. While in the far corner next to the window, the television set was going. Every now and then the curtain would flutter from the soft breeze that blew every so often. I would look up to catch a few glimpses of tv as they chatted away. Jackie! come on and eat, I heard my mother say from the kitchen.

I rose from the floor and went into the kitchen where she was. The living room was an open room with its smoke-filled wallpaper, that at one time used to be bright and airy with delightful patches of flowers now rustic and dark, the other half of the wall was painted dirty antique white paint. Had a long navy -blue couch, the bedroom equipped with a twin bed and chair.

The kitchen had one window with a fire escape attached, then there was the stove, refrigerator, table and front door. The whole place had an ominous look to it, except the kitchen, where I went to climb into my seat at the table. I wasn't the typical gulp my food down quick kind of kid, I ate rather slow, pausing every now and then to dream. I would catch visions right in the middle of doing something.

My mind would just go with it. I had managed to eat everything except my carrots, I remember thinking to myself,

"I'm going to save this for last". But I'd become full by the time I ate everything else. So, I climbed down and went told my mother that I was finished eating, she was laying down in the bed at this time, I made my way to her and triumphantly announced to her that I was finished eating.

Good she said, now did you eat all your carrots? I felt depleted, because she wasn't happy that I had finished like a good girl, the way that I had envisioned. Saddened I shook my head no, just stood there. My mother ordered me back to my plate to eat my carrots, I went back and I sat there what seemed like a long time, as I played with them on my plate, I lined them up, I stacked them, I cut them up.

Slowly but surely, I began to get sleepy. Knowing my mother wouldn't let me get up without finishing them, so I shoved them all into my mouth, so many until I was about to puke when I remembered what was in my mouth. Ugh! I'd think to myself, as I sat cheeks full of nasty carrots, dreaming as I frequently did, when out of the distance I heard my mother call me.

I climbed down and went to her, cheeks still full of carrots, I answered her as best as I could. She had me sit in the chair in the bedroom. So, I sat there. My mother told me, "when you finish those carrots, then you can come to bed" I sat with food in my mouth for as long as I could. Sleepily as I was, I just couldn't muster the strength to chew and swallow the nasty stuff.

Hoping she would get tired and tell me to go and spit it out, but that never came. Still I sat there. Sleep was coming heavy now, cheeks full like a squirrel, my head bobbed side to side, back & forth. Then my mother yelled at me, "Swallow that food Jackie! I'd jumped out of fear, started crying at first a soft sniffle and whimper for a few minutes until she had gotten tired of my noise, then she'd roar at me!

"Swallow it or you're getting a whipping!", that was scary to me, because that meant she was angry, and when she was angry that usually meant I was going to get a beating from her, for some infraction of sorts. In this case disobedience for not swallowing my carrots. Just out of fear alone I openly cried, mouth still full of food, not being able to fully breathe through my mouth.

I would gag in between breaths, cough and gurgle my food. Before I knew it, she was out of the bed with a belt, and she'd beat me, stinging me on my legs and arms, my hand and feet, all caught the belt before I went to sleep that night. A few days later, I again was in the living room with my mother, she on the couch watching tv I was on the floor, busy entertaining myself with whatever I could find.

When suddenly my mother announced she was leaving to go outside for a while, and that she would be back. I looked at her, and shook my head up and down, and said yeah. I knew from previous experience not to do certain things, because my mother gets angry. She said to me, don't you open that door for nobody, do you hear me? Again, I looked at her wide eyed and shook my head yes. Then she left.

I continued to play with whatever I could find on the floor, my imagination did the rest, the tv was on as I looked around, I remember thinking that she wasn't back, I wondered where she could be? So, I kept on playing, time had gotten away, when suddenly there was a knock at the door, I just sat there at first, it kept on knocking and knocking. I had gotten up and went to the door thinking it was my mother, I said mommy?

That's when I heard a voice say Jackie! It's me? Open the door? Trying to help my mother I pulled on the door, and it came open, but instead of my mother it was my aunt Gloria. She didn't come inside, she just asked me, is your mother home? Where is your Mother? I just shook my head, then Gloria told me to stay here, she shut the door and then left. I went back to playing in the living room, when my mother came in the door a little while later after that.

She came into the house asking if anybody came by, I shook my head yeah. She asked me in a probing voice who was it? I didn't answer, so she called a few names when she had gotten to Gloria's name, I shook my head yeah. Immediately my mother wanted to know if I had let her in, did you open the door? I shook my head yeah, then she left back out, then she came back and said to me "Didn't I tell you!" Not" to open that door?" Is that not what I said?"

I just looked at her dazed and confused, again she said even louder, her anger building to a feverish pitch "DIDN'T I TELL YOU?" as she walked into the bedroom to find her belt, I watched as she reappeared with belt in hand, with the look of stern discipline in her eye, I immediately started to cry as she approached me with the belt raised above her head, it swooshed thru the air as it connected to my flesh.

It felt like a hot knife slicing straight through to the bone. She kept repeating it over & over again, "Didn't I Tell you" whack after whack!. I screamed and screamed crying from the stings and pings, I'd try to run, but she would grab my arm and kept on swinging the belt onto my legs, my back, lower torso, and feet. I would jump and try to kick away at the leather belt that would come down on my skin in rapid fire.

But try as I may, she had a vice grip on my arm, that no matter which way I tried to run, I was NOT getting away! Then she readjusted her grip when she grabbed me by the back of my neck, and shoved my head between her legs, pinning me down, and continued to whack my backside. It felt like peals of lightning strikes with each whack! The pain was quite sharp and intense as it landed with such precision.

When she suddenly stopped, I just lay slumped on the floor, crying profusely, and writhing in intense pain. Thinking, rather hoping it was over, I could only watch as she stormed over and commenced to rip the tv cord out of the wall. Grimacing, staring right at me, began to wrap the cord tightly around her wrist, and beat me with the extension cord! Lash after painstaking lash! If you have never experienced being hit with an electrical cord before?

It is 5x's worse than a belt! The force used to whip the cord, then add to that the distance from the object plays a large role in the severity of the pain. Then, add to that its molecular, plastic structure which is basically the covering for a couple wires or quite a few, depending on its usage. Tends to leave different markings on the skin, Shows up on the flesh as deep bruising or whelps on the skin.

Quite capable of cutting through the flesh. In describing the intense pain. I can tell you it feels like a severely hot branding iron! In the case of a child, being lashed by an adult, well let's just say, it's as brutal as one can get. As she fiercely continued to whip the cord, she would unwind it from time to time in order to gain more distance between us, flexing it to inflict as much pain as she possibly could, again, and again!

Not caring in the least where the cord would strike me, my back, legs, face, head, eyes she showed absolutely no mercy whatsoever! I screamed deafening screams. Louder and louder at the pain, out of nowhere there was a faint knock at the door, it kept getting louder, then there was banging on the door. Abruptly she stopped whacking me and moved through the living room toward the kitchen to investigate the knocking at the door.

I was still crying, I looked over into the kitchen, I could see my mother tussling and wrestling with someone at the door. Then my aunt Glory emerged from the kitchen, walking toward me, she scooped me up off the floor and carried me out of my mother's apartment. Carrying me straight to my grandmother. They called the police, who then took me to the hospital, Johns Hopkins pediatrics emergency room.

The doctors and nurse couldn't believe their eyes! Then and there, the decision was made to take me away from my mother. They questioned how a mother could be, such a monster toward a human being was beyond their scope of imagination and, understanding. They knew, and have known evil exist, but this far exceeded their depth of comprehension, and set the bar at a whole new level.

Each were saddened and angered to take immediate action, on behalf of this innocent soul before them. Not only did they give my relatives instructions on how to nurse me back to health but also, the necessary steps through the court proceedings, how to petition the courts for full custody. From that tragic night up to the court date, my grandmother was temporary custody of me.

I lived with her, and had grown accustomed to her schedule, I slept beside my grandmother, in her bed, one night while I was sleeping, I was wakened by a great disruption going on in the house, I had gotten out of bed. Went and peeked around the bedroom corner into the living room, there I saw my uncle Paul and my mother Hope engaged in battle! Sister against brother squaring off, my mother had her infamous broken glass bottle wielding it like a sword.

In the middle of my grandmothers living room! I could tell my mother had been drinking, by the way she was talking, she had a pronounced drunken slur. I looked at my uncle, his white shirt was disheveled, and torn, like he was in a brawl. He was intently staring at my mother, locked and loaded, watching her every move! I could see my grandmother, she was standing inside the doorway of her kitchen and her living room, on the opposite side of the apartment.

She had a look of fear in her eyes, watching helplessly as her 2 kids fought in her house. I had no idea what was going on, all I knew was that I didn't want to go back with my mother, and I hoped that they wouldn't let her take me away. While they fought, I ran over to my grandmother, and held onto her. My mother managed to cut my uncle across his chest with the glass, immediately he bled.

When my mother saw his flesh open, she promptly exited her mother's apartment before the police were called. A couple of days had gone by, my grandmother fixed my hair, dressed me and took me to the courthouse. We sat in the audience until her name was called, she picked me up and walked up to the judge. He motioned to come up to his desk and she sat me there to talk with him personally.

He asked me a few questions, eyeballing my still fresh wounds, "Do you remember who did this to you?" I quietly shook my head in a yes motion. He asked me directly "Who did that to you? "My mommy" I said quietly! He said a few words to my grandmother, then asked me who did I want to be with? I pointed to my grandmother. It wasn't long after that, it became official, the judge made his ruling, that I would be in my grandmother's custody, Permanently.

Most of the time I slept and ate, I was still quiet, but my grandmother knew how to reach me, communicate with me. I grew to love and trust her completely. I was eating regularly, sleeping normal times, being cared for, I was getting used to a consistent routine living like a normal kid. My cousin would come over from time to time, she was slightly older than I, and would show me things she learned, like tying my shoes, making rabbit ears.

Which took quite a few tries, but I eventually caught on. Soon it was time to go to school. My grandmother enrolled me into Colington Square Elementary School. There a boy took a liking to me, named Daniel, he wasn't my classmate but attended the same school I attend. Daily after school, he would chase me home, I would run like the wind those 3 blocks, all the way to my grandmother's house.

Run up the steps, and slammed the front door shut, ran up the steps to her apartment, breathing heavily like I ran a 10 mi. marathon. My grandmother would ask me" child what's wrong with you?" Still scared and breathing heavily, I'd say mama that boy won't leave me alone. What boy? She'd ask, I'd say him? pointing outside, she would go look out the window, but he would be long gone by then. Ok she'd say, and we would drop the subject.

The next few days the exact same thing would happen, one day I came sprinting home, from school, with him running close behind. She was looking out the window when I came running up the steps, bam! Slammed the door shut behind me. The following day same thing, here I come like the wind, running as fast as I could, I bent the corner and ran up the steps. To my horror, the door was locked tight, I pushed on it, and it wouldn't budge!

I looked up at the window, and she yelled down to me" fight him"! You better kick his --------! I ran down the steps, to look up to the window, begging my grandmother, when I turned around, he was coming up to me, and I immediately started swinging like a wildcat.

Chapter 2

It was all adrenaline and fear! That poor kid never gotten a punch in edgewise. My grandmother had come downstairs, to watched me fight him in front of her door. When we were done, he went his way, and I went up to my grandmother. We walked up the steps together, and nothing else was said. I felt good though, real proud of myself! Needless to say, he didn't chase me again after that.

About a month later my grandmother moved into a new place, in a totally different neighborhood. We moved to an area called Westport, in the Cherryhill area in south Baltimore, close to the rear of the Chesapeake Bay. In a sub-division, street named Dorton Court. Its frequently known as a city housing development, for low income families. She took me and enrolled me into the elementary school in the area.

During the winter seasons in the 1970's you hardly knew people lived in these communities. It was very serene and quiet for the most part. The summer seasons were a different story, however. There were your average ruffians, but they stayed in their own communities for the most part, every now and again we would hear of some tough clans across the tracks, but they stayed across the tracks.

This allowed the youngsters to come outside and play, all day until the sun went down, and even then, during the summer when there wasn't any school. Kids didn't have to go into their homes until well after 10oclock pm. That was purely at the discretion of the families. My grandmother didn't play that, she made it clear I was to be in the house when the sun went down, no questions asked. I was obedient and did what she said.

Families moved into the neighborhood almost daily, it was exciting times, because that meant more kids to play with. The adults were friendly toward one another and watched each other's kids from time to time. Whenever the parent announced they weren't going to be home. I blossomed into a typical kid, I thoroughly enjoyed interactive sports, and picking teammates, being competitive, in team associated games.

My grandmother kept tight reigns on me and didn't let me get too far out of her sight. From time to time us girls would play with our barbie dolls, dress up, do their hair, on each other's tiny 3 step front stoop. They also taught me how to play jacks, once I really began to learn how to play, I had gotten extremely good at it. I would look for another challenge. When I had gotten a little taller my grandmother started sending me to the corner store.

I would get her favorites, which were a pack of Kool's cigarettes, and a coke soda. Which then in that era only cost about 0.35 total. Boy, how times have changed! I would go and come back with no problem. I would also use this time as an opportunity to sight see, some days if I was feeling sad, I would look for my biological father. Once when I was about to cross Westview, a busy intersection, headed to the corner store.

I saw the transit bus turning the corner, and the driver waved to me, I immediately imagined that was him. Not all my friends' families had both parents, but those that did, for obvious reasons I would sometimes wonder what it was like, to have both parents, or was it was better having only one? For the most part

I only played with my classmates, and immediate neighbors, and their families. My extended family members would come to my grandmother's house.

Primarily on Friday or Saturday nights, My aunts, uncles, and their friends from area bars and local hang out spots, would come to my grandmother's place, which was fast becoming the hang out spot to gather, laugh, drink, dance and have all kinds of fun together. Then they would leave, go someplace else. For me, it was exciting to see my other family members, they would always inquire about how I was doing.

If they were feeling really generous, they would sometimes give me a dollar, and I would run outside and spend it with my neighborhood buddies. On the ice cream truck that came through all of the neighborhoods, and sold, ice cream of all flavors and sizes, assorted candy, sodas, juices etc. My family was big on instilling certain behavioral rules that kids should stay in a kid's place, which only meant, my interaction with them should be limited.

That I should not sit among them, drinking, smoking cigarettes and using swear words like they do. Living with my grandmother was the one and only place that I remember having a stable home and family life, wasn't always the greatest but it was home. Her house was a typical two-story townhouse, walking into the front door is the kitchen which had one window, a kitchen table, her washing machine, sink, counter, cupboards, and a pantry.

Then there is the living room, a closet to the left, only big enough to hang 3 coats, and store a few toys. Wall to the stairwell, back door, window and a nice sized living room, a picture with a stormy cloud, with a bleak, lighted opening in the cloud, in the sky, leaving to the imagination, I assumed that's where God lived.

A component set. Upstairs at the very top was the bathroom, next to the bathroom was a linen closet, made inside the wall.

Then there was her room, then my room. My Grandmother worked, as a high school janitor during the day. She made it clear that I would be alone, at least until she gets home. When she wasn't home, I would eat whatever I could find, watch tv, play alone take a nap, or curiously rummage through her belongings. She would come in the house and flop down in the living room on the couch kick off her shoes and call me.

I would be upstairs pretending with my toys. I would always go see how she was doing, see if she needed me to do anything for her. I so loved to sit and talk with her, or just look in her face, she was a dark skinned older woman, she kept her hair in a short afro blowout, when she smiled she would show perfect teeth, with a shiny gold tooth on the side. Those teeth weren't her real ones though, but to me she had a smile that made the sun jealous.

A heart that was even bigger than it. She would always ask me are you hungry? I so loved her cooking, I would jump up in my happy glee and run with her to the kitchen, saying yes, ma'am! I would sit at the table to watch her as she got different items ready, she would go in and out of the pantry for this and that, all the while talking to me, we would laugh at her jokes, and I would try my hand at one or two.

She would take her teeth out, and send me upstairs to stick them in her jar, that she had in the mirror medicine cabinet, and I'd run back downstairs. Living with her I found out, she was a deep believer in GOD & Jesus, and she loved talking to me about them. While she talked, I could see her beam, her eyes would twinkle, she was infectious, watching and listening to her talk made me feel alive.

Her commitment, her devotion and compassion about the word of GOD was unmistakable. Her favorite evangelist was Jimmy Swagger. I don't think she missed an episode back in the 70's.

He would come on tv every Sunday morning, and she would have her huge big black bible right there so she could diligently follow along. When he wasn't on tv, she would find occasions to tell me about GOD & Jesus's journey on earth, and I would sit and listen.

Just to be in her company, feeling her love and attention was priceless to me. Watching her enjoy her favorite topic even without her teeth, in my eyes it made her look much more childlike herself. As she talked away I would dream of a time that I would take care of her, Not because I had to or out of a deep sense of obligation and duty, but because I deeply desired to demonstrate to her how valuable and meaningful she is to me.

It would only be a small fraction of what she gives to me daily. As she continued to cook and talk, I would listen and ask questions too, sometimes my questions were so thought provoking to her that it would take her a minute to respond. To process my question, I would patiently wait like a good student. While I waited, she would pass me a potato and show me how to peel it with a potato peeler, and she would eventually answer my question, and talk some more.

Dinner was done and we ate, I would "ooh and ahh" at her food, and she would jokingly say to me "Girl you sure can eat"! and we would laugh. I'd help clean the table off, and afterward ask to go outside. She would allow it, I think mostly because she wanted to continue unwinding from work or talk on the phone with my Aunt Gloria. When I would come in to use the bathroom or get a drink of water, I could hear her talking, laughing or giggling.

They were very close and told each other everything. While outside I would go looking for kids that I could play with, and if I couldn't find anybody, I would go across the street to Mrs. Dorothy's place. She was an older lady my grandmother had befriended, since moving into the neighborhood, now we kind of treat her like family. Mrs. Dorothy is a believer too, and she is someone my grandmother shared bible study with.

Her son lives with her, and they have a dog name tang, she's a chihuahua. I sat with Mrs. Dorothy from time to time while she watched tv while lying in her king-sized bed, if she needed anything I would go downstairs and get it for her. Her favorite item was a tall glass of ice water.

When I grew bored, I would wander downstairs through her living room and look at her family portraits, and her son Butch, when he was a little boy.

Except he's not so little anymore. It always amazed me how much people changed from photos. He went from a little skinny dark- skinned kid, to this chunky fat overweight teenager. Butch-y, as he liked to be called, was about 17 yrs. of age, he had bowlegs and walked pigeon toed, and had a come- hither walk. I used to think it was funny to see him coming, because he would always be sweating, like it was painful to walk from being so overweight.

Out of curiosity I asked him one day, "what's wrong with you?" I had been wanting to ask that question, and his response to me was" I'm a fag!" he would announce. The way he said that to me, was loaded with ownership. I didn't fully grasp what that meant. But if it didn't feel good in my internal compass, I'd just assumed it was probably wrong on some level. Eventually I would find my way back home.

I came in the door and head upstairs to get ready for bed, my grandmother was in her room, she yelled out go ahead and run your bathwater, I did just that most of the time I just sat and played with my toys in the tub, or just sit quietly. When I grew listless, sleepy I would get out and go into my grandmothers' room. To find a shirt to sleep in, we would talk for a little bit, then sleepily tell me to go get into your bed.

I would leave her and head to my room. Living with her was like we were 2 peas in a pod, I looked to her for everything. She was the matriarch of the family, the strength and backbone that held us all together. Her kids had a great deal of respect for her, well most of them anyway. They made it known, under no uncertain terms that I was to do the same. Personally, I don't think anyone had more respect for her than I did.

Morning came and mama had gotten up, if there were anything extra, she needed me to do, and she felt that I could do it for her, she would call me to her and tell me. This morning mama had gotten up for work, she called me, and I went to her, she told me, " I have to work, if any mail come, I want you to put all my mail on the table, ok?, don't leave it on the floor anymore" Yes mam" I would say:

Immediately to associate exactly what she wanted, I would picture it in my mind, whatever she requested of me. I turned around and went back into my room. Back to sleep until I woke up on my own, I would wander through the house, until it dawned on me that I was home alone. I would turn the tv on sit down to look at the cartoons, then when I had gotten hungry, I would go to the kitchen and look through the refrigerator to find something to eat.

Anything from leftovers from dinner, to putting together a peanut butter & jelly sandwich, then run back to take my seat on the floor, to continue watching the tv shows. My favorite was Popeye the sailor man, Josie & The Pussy cats, Speed racer, Bugs bunny & friends, Captain Chesapeake, Gilligan's island. Out of nowhere I would hear somebody at the front door, I sat completely still and listened.

Then I would see the mail being pushed through the mail-slot and hit the floor.

I would get up and scoop up the mail and put them on the kitchen table. I'd run back to the tv, until I had gotten bored. I would go upstairs and busy myself with finding something to play with, using my vivid imagination with my toys. Then I would go back downstairs, stopped short of the this long oblong wooden box.

Situated beside the back door next to the living room window, It had smooth dark wood, on the top, resembling a table. Along the front edge of it was a way to lift the top off, investigating further I opened the lid, and inside it had 2 sides, one of which had a circular platform with a mechanical arm attached to it, for playing 33's sized disc shaped albums, for a series of songs, and 45's sized disc shaped for playing a single song in particular.

The other side was the radio, and several knobs and a dial for setting to a specified station.

AM or FM, radio stations my family's favorite radio station was 1300 WEBB, that played music all day, as well as various artist that made music history. Artist like Stevie Wonder whose career had taken off into the stratosphere, Lou Rawls, Patti Labelle, and others blared through the airwaves regularly.

My favorite artist back then was Lisa Stansfield, and her song was "All around the world".

I randomly selected the record, picked up the 45 single and placed it on the record player, lifted the needle onto the record, and listened to her croon. Over and over again I played that song, memorizing the words, until I learned every word to that song, next I mimicked her voice, her tones, pitches, the lows and highs.

Until I could sing her song all the way to the end, word for word, and range for range.

I was transformed into her world, as if I were standing in the very same room with her, somehow, we merged. Now it was me singing, as if I'd became her. I had disappeared and became a spectator among the captivated audience. It all came effortlessly in my mind and body I was an entertainer. When I grew bored, I would look around and find other things to investigate.

When my grandmother came home from work, I had made a little mess. She would ask me "what were you doing all day?" I would tell her everything except listening to music and trying my hand at singing. As she sat on the couch, I would bounce next to her, and ask a bunch of questions about her day, as we talked, she would kick off her shoes, loosen her top and bottom false teeth, spit them out into her hands, hand them to me, then send me upstairs to the bathroom medicine cabinet, where she kept a tall glass of water,"

Here take these upstairs," she'd say. Yes mam, and off I would go. I would drop each one in the tall glass, eyeballing them carefully. Examining them like, some science experiment, carefully observing them, I'd watch as the bottom teeth would sort of float at an angle, with the top teetering at some awkward distorted distance off to the side. In all this I had completely forgotten she was home, even waiting for me to come back downstairs.

In being totally consumed by her teeth, I had ended up taking them back out of the cup and placing them up to my mouth, observing immediately that they were way too wide for my face.

I didn't care I mimicked my grandmother's laughter, moving the teeth as I spoke with each word, until I heard my grandmother call for me downstairs," What are you doing up there girl?" jogging me out of my fantasy state.

I hurriedly put them back into the medicine cabinet and shut the door. By the time I had gotten downstairs, she was already in the kitchen, as I walked in, she was opening her mail, tossing a few off to the side. I climbed into the chair at the table, I would sit and watch her every move, her facial expressions were interesting to me. She was very expressive, talking to me watching her face told me how she was feeling at that moment in time.

I'd sit and observe it all, her tone of voice, her mannerisms. I watched her take particular interest in a specific piece of mail. Eyes widened with excitement she triumphantly announced, with her big wide toothless grin, "Here we go" she said, holding it up proudly, she pushed it across the table, in my direction, this one's for you! With an air of pride and love. I reached for it with innocent glee and astonishment, asking in high- pitched excitement.

"What's this mama? I asked, she said "it's a letter from the church Jackie look! they wrote you.!! I was grinning too, looking at the envelope, at the thought of somebody writing to me, and what that could mean. She had written the church on my behalf, and they responded in kind, she told me "go ahead open the letter?!" Getting up out of her chair she came over to me, to point out in the letter, that they had addressed me directly,

See look! She said, as she pointed to the bold letters on the opening statement. I can't tell you how good that made me feel, like I was somebody special. As if I wasn't moving fast enough.

She began reading the letter to me, as I held it in my hands I listened intently, she stopped periodically to explain to me the definitions of certain words to me, like Hallelujah, Glorified, Salvation.

How these same words were in the Bible, that she reads. Some of it sounded familiar to me. simply because she would share some of her understanding with me. To further illustrate what Pastor Swagger was saying is indeed true, she quickly sent me upstairs to get her Bible, hurry up she'd say! Run upstairs and look on my desk and get me that big black book, you've seen me reading.

Yes mam, I would say, and I would go and get it for her, but of course I had to look at it first, flip through a page or two, before I headed for the stairs. I would sit in my seat and listen to her tell me about GOD, Jesus and The Holy Spirit while she cooked dinner. My brain was very inquisitive as I grew in every way, soaking up information, from everything. We ate, and as usual I would be in a hurry to get outside.

She taught me, in her patient way how to help with the cleaning of the kitchen, clean off the table, put dishes in the sink, learn how to wash the dishes.

CHAPTER 3

At first, I was to stand there and watch her do it, then she would stand aside and coach me. When we were done, I was ready to run around with my neighborhood friends. I would go and find them, and they would continue to teach me how to play jacks, starting out with one at a time then progressing to ten, which consisted of all of them at once.

Or, playing with each other's dolls or playing hopscotch. I always had a grand time playing, it was the only time where I could be a kid, carefree and wanton. There seemed to never be a shortage of games to play. We played until the sun went down, and I would head home. When I came in, I heard her calling for me, so I went upstairs to her room to see what she wanted, Mam? I'd ask?"

I have to take you to get shots for school tomorrow, so take a bath and get ready for bed" she said. Yes mam, and I went into the bathroom, and ran my water, as I sat in the tub, I started to think about the shots, and wondered if it would hurt. I sat there for a while, playing with my toys. When I was done, I went and found me a shirt from my grandmother, then climbed into my bed. The next morning, she called to me and I woke up, she told me to get dressed.

Grab you a shirt, and some pants from the closet. When I couldn't find what she wanted, she came in and fished around in the pile of clothes on the floor, and found an outfit for me, and put some decent ponytails in my hair, and we left out the back door. Headed to the school, she instructed me that this is the path to take to go to school daily, that she would not always be around to hold my hand, and that I would have do things on my own.

Walking, I listened intently as she spoke, about what was going to happen, if the shot hurt really bad to just squeeze her hand. And just what she expected of me. Yes mam, I would say. We arrived at the nurse's office, and we took a seat until it was our turn to go inside. She took the seat and I stood next to her, as she talked with the nurse. When the nurse was ready, she picked up the needle, complete with a tiny bottle with liquid inside, and asked if I was ready?

No, I said, looking wide eyed, directly at the needle, my grandmother pulled me close to her, and slid me onto her lap, in a bear hug, the lady took my arm and pricked it, injecting the shot, and took some blood as well. I cried of course, but when we were done, my grandmother gave me a proud hug and kiss, and the nurse gave me a lollipop on the promise that I stopped crying. Then we left and went back home.

On our walk back home, my grandmother reminded me about our previous conversation, the paths I would take, and how I will be ok. She would ask me, "Are you ok Jackie? I'd shake my head up and down in a yes, with lollipop in my mouth, and residual tears still in my eyes. We headed home where she would then start frying some chicken, boy I loved how it smelled, as she would cook, she would make conversation out of anything, I would just sit there and listen.

We would eat, and I would help out in the kitchen, then head outside to play. My first day of school, was full of testing, to see where I would be placed, what I knew academically, and didn't know. Ultimately, they placed me in 1st grade, during class I would have a series of what I liked to call mind journeys. There were times when I was fully engaged in school, and times I were not and would give way to my imagination.

It was during these times my mind was most busy with fragments of things or pictures I would see, things I couldn't immediately associate with. School didn't really require much interaction anyway, I could let my mind wander, as long, as I wasn't being disruptive, the teacher didn't care. I would sit quietly and play with the toys that was allowed, for hours upon hours until lunch time.

We would all line up in a single line, and walk over to the other building, because my class was in the trailer, outside on the playground, and from the trailer we would walk over to the school building to the cafeteria for lunch. The same back to the trailer for the remainder of the day, until it was time to go home. Day after day, just like my grandmother told me, I would walk this same route, back and forth to school.

One day, headed to school, I decided to go a different path, which was to cut through an alley, behind the houses that face the street, the schools property was fenced off, I'd walk to the very end of the fence, turning aside into the school yard. The same was repeated at the end of the day, when I went home. Entered through the backdoor, and that's where I stayed until she got home from work. I was to change clothes and do my homework.

Eat, and watch a little tv. As I was watching tv, my grandmother came in the door, and sat heavily down on the couch, she had me pull her shoes off, and gently rub her feet, I listened as she complained of how much they ached. I would sit on the floor and rub her feet until they felt better. When she was ready, she would pluck her teeth out, and send me upstairs to the medicine cabinet, while she started dinner.

"We got company in a little while, everybody is coming over," she said, I'd responded yes mam. While I was outside, I would casually look up and see my relatives all pulling up in vehicles with their friends. My uncle Paul also pulls up in his hotrod car, which was a big black dodge, complete with the fat rear tires. When I came inside to see who all was there, I saw my baby brother for the first time, in a long time.

Sitting in the living room, she was hugging her grandson, she announced that he would be coming to stay with us. Happily, I stood beside my grandmother, I held my little brothers' hand, a 1 yr. old chunky little light skinned boy, gripped my finger. By the time I ran back outside, there were other carloads of people, coming to be with my grandmother. There was a man among the people, who turned out to be her boyfriend, his name was Mr. Frank.

She invited him over to meet the family, hang out with them for the day. They all sat around, talking, and pulling out their drinks, He brought some freshly fried squirrel with him, and gave it to my grandmother. She gave me and my little brother some, had us sit down at the table to eat. While we were eating, my grandmother looked over at me, and asked" How's that chicken you're eating?" I said mmm, mmm good! Chewing a piece off the bone, I sure do love your chicken mama! I exclaimed

She paused a moment while my lips were busy smacking, then said, uh. That's not chicken that you're eating right now! It took a second to register what she was saying, slowing down my chewing, wrinkling my forehead and eyebrows quite bewildered "it's not"? I responded, shaking her head, side to side Nope! she said, as informative as she could, Its squirrel! Like it? I made an ugly face, as the realization came to view in my mind what a squirrel is.

I envisioned this little furry, fluffy tailed vermin running from tree to tree! She said "yup!", with a big smug wide grin on her face. Good isn't it? Yes mam, I responded, slowly with far less enthusiasm as before. I ate everything on my plate, except what was left of the squirrel. She and Mr. Frank just looked at me and they both giggled. When I was done, I asked could I go back outside, and finish playing with my friends.

She agreed to let me, but told me to take your brother with you. I took him by the hand, and led the way, I felt so much like the big sister that day, I took him and introduced him to everybody outside, all my friends saw my little brother, he went everywhere with me. Every move I made, he tagged along. We went back inside, so I could use the bathroom, when I came back downstairs, he was with my grandmother.

She was laughing, talking, having a great time. They saw me, and asked me to dance the latest dance for them, so I did, and when I was done, I ran back outside to catch up with my friends who were busy catching lightning bugs out back, dismembering them, by detaching the lighted belly of the bugs, and putting the glowing belly on their earlobes and donning them as earrings. They would stay lit for quite some time, long enough to make designs out of them too.

We would play tag and other childhood games. Only when I wore myself out did I find my way home again. I came in through the back door, the party was over, and everybody had disappeared, I could hear my grandmother, who was out front, talking. So, I started cleaning up in the living room, beer cans, liquor bottles, ash trays littered the living room. I threw all the trash away, then went to the front door, calling for my grandmother.

She answered, "what? I'm out here" she said, opening the front door, I told her ma, I cleaned up, the living room. She just said "good, go head on to bed, and don't wake your brother"! Yes mam. I went upstairs, and climbed into my bed, looking over at my little brother, who was sound asleep. I was glad he is here with me. A little later, I heard her shut the front door, then coming up the steps.

She peeked into our room, then opened her bedroom door, and went to bed. The next morning, when I woke up, my little brother Justice was just sitting there looking around, so I walked over to him and picked him up out of bed, and walked him down the steps, to the living room. I turned the tv on for us to watch, and he sat there with me, it was the first time that I had really gotten a good look at him, and I could still see the scar that was on his top lip.

I had gotten up to fix us a bowl of cereal, gave it to him to sit and eat by himself while we were watching early morning cartoons. When my grandmother came downstairs. She told us" to go outside if we wanted to, while she watched tv". Yes mam, I took my brother outside to play. We joined the other kids outside, ripping & running up and down the block. Stopping to come inside only to drink water, use the bathroom, or eat.

Later that same week, after school we all were outside playing. When I saw someone older than I waving to me, and calling for me, so I went to see what they wanted, they asked me could I go to the store, for them. I did the same thing for my grandmother all the time, so it wasn't an unusual request. So, I politely agreed, I stood there patiently waiting for him to hand me the money, with a note attached or something.

He reached out, I could see the money in his hand, so I reached out to take the money when I opened my hand that's when he grabbed me by the hand, grabbed my arm and yanked me inside their door so fast, by the time a sound made it out of my vocal chords, I was already inside of their house. Standing off to the side of the door and out of view, was another person, an older boy about 17 or 18!

The one who pulled me inside, covered my mouth, preventing me from screaming or yelling, all in one swift motion, I had no time to react, desperately trying to call my grandmother, he picked me up and slammed me on the floor. With me writhing, kicking and squirming, he pulled my shorts off, instructed the boy to hold my hands over my head, out of his way while he climbed on top of me with all his weight holding my legs firmly out of the way.

He entered himself inside of my vagina, out of nowhere the pain shot through me, like a bolt of lightning, I screamed blood curdling screams into the hands of the one holding my mouth! The pain between my legs, was fiery & intense, for what seemed like a very long time as he mercilessly jammed himself inside of me time after time, after time, with each pounding stroke, felt like a knife cutting deeper & deeper inside of me, as I bled.

It wasn't until he was done with me, when he jumped up off of me, that I was able to roll over to prop myself up off the floor, that's when the boy that was holding my hands, wanted his turn, and he pushed me back down to the floor, this time on my stomach. The one had just finished is now holding my hands. The other one, then forced his way inside of my rear anal cavity! It was intense excruciating pain.

I think I passed out! He still entered me and was having his way with me! For what seemed like a very long time. When he finished, before I knew it, they took me to the back door, pushed me outside, and shut the door. My whole body was on fire, especially between my legs.

I went home, which was only a few doors down, but it seemed like it took me forever to finally get there. I had found a way to walk, that didn't hurt so bad.

I walked in, and went straight upstairs, my stomach, between my legs, and rear end were throbbing aching so intensely, I climbed into my bed, cried myself to sleep. Out of nowhere I heard my grandmother call me, just like she had so many times before. I had gotten up to go see what she wanted, went downstairs to see her, she was talking to me, asking me why didn't I have on any clothes?

I didn't hear her, angrily she demanded to know "what's wrong with you"? she told me to come up to her, when I did, that's when she asked me, "Why are you walking like that"? with my head held down, all I could say was, "they held me down!" The fact is, I didn't know I was walking different, all I knew was the pain was like fire between my legs, would not go away. I was walking trying to keep my vagina lips, and inner thighs from rubbing together.

I was bloody, everything was so intensely bruised, which was evidence that something terrible had happened to me. My grandmother asked me forcibly Who?... who did that to you? I told her, in a low voice the boys a few doors up did it and wouldn't let me go! All she could say to me was, go take a bath! I made my way up the steps to run my bath water. I sat there, just sat there for a long time, not fully able to comprehend what just occurred and why? Why did this have to happen to me? The house was quiet, everything was eerily still, it was like time had stilled itself also. In listening I could hear a ringing in my head. All I wanted to do was hide myself. I couldn't process this horrifying event.

I walked into my room and l crawled into bed. My little brother came into the house, into the room and wanted me to come outside, but I didn't budge from the bed, where I felt safe. I was no longer the brave warrior, big sister, the chosen one to protect my little brother, that I used to be now it is I who need protecting. My grandmother told everybody what happened to me, there was not one soul that didn't know that I was raped.

To me she said, "from now on, after school, you and your brother are to go to Mrs. Dorothy's and stay there until I get off work. I quietly agreed, yes mam. Some time had passed before I felt safe enough to go back outside and play again. Before I could walk and run and play normally. They say time heals all wounds. The weekend rolled around again, and my family brought their friends over for drinks and to have a good time.

We were outside playing hard, when the sun went down, we came in the house, the party was over. I immediately started cleaning up the beer cans, beer cups, and liquor bottles that were left behind, and full ashtrays I began emptying them in the trash. I continued to clean up, when I heard footsteps coming down the steps, it was Mr. Frank, but I kept on cleaning, moving around, back a forth to the trash can.

When he saw that I was coming back to the living room, he stood in the way, I tried to walk around him, that's when he took my hand, and pulled me close to him, bending down to kiss me

Chapter 4

Pulling me so close I could smell the liquor on his hot breath, but I jerked away in fear and shrieked, so loud my grandmother, who was sitting outside heard me, she called for me Jackie?, Mam! I responded while running to the front door.

In looking backward, he put his finger up to his lips, I caught a glimpse before I opened the door, my grandmother asked me "what's wrong"? before I could utter a word out of my mouth, Mr. Frank had reached the door too, over talking me, interrupting our conversation. He started talking to my grandmother, so I backed, up into the house and went upstairs to my bed. I looked over and saw that my brother was asleep.

Eventually I fell off to sleep too. The next morning, I woke up and went downstairs, my little brother followed me. We sat on the floor watching tv, when I got hungry, I got up and fixed he and I some cereal in a bowl, we were eating when my grandmother and Mr. Frank both came downstairs. She began cooking breakfast, we all ate at the table it was then that I learned he also work, and moved in with us.

My birthday rolled around, my great uncle Clint bought me a bike, took me out back, and taught me how to balance myself on the bike, while pedaling it. After I learned, then I taught my little brother how to ride a bike too. One morning came, and as usual I could half hear my grandmother get up to leave for work, in my sleep, sometime shortly thereafter, Mr. Frank came into our room.

Picked me up and took me into my grandmother's room, lay me down in her bed, and he lay beside me. When I finally arose from my slumber, opened my eyes, I saw his face so close to mine, smiling at me saying to me "Good morning beautiful! As soon as he spoke those creepy words to me, I cringed from the horrible stench of his breath, reminiscent of the neighborhood dumpster at its foulest on a scorching hot summer day.

The smell of rancid debris emanating from it, made your nose hairs curl, immediately I covered my mouth and nose with my hand, saying" Ugh" Mr. Frank!, your breath stinks! he seemed surprised by my statement, and was slightly taken aback, saying to me, "It do?" oh wait a minute, he jumped up, and opened the bedroom door, and went into the bathroom, and brushed his teeth, I lay there wondering how did

I get here? Then he came back into the room, as he shut the bedroom door, he stood looking proudly at me, climbing back into the bed, beside me, saying now, where was I? When suddenly we heard my little brother get up, and whining at the bedroom door. I had gotten out of the bed and left Mr. Frank to take my little brother downstairs so we could eat breakfast and watch tv. While we watched tv, Mr. Frank came downstairs, and quietly left the house.

We stayed inside until my grandmother came home. I did not tell my grandmother what happened that morning, right way. I believe I was afraid that she wouldn't believe me, the same was said about me to myself, I really was confused, and couldn't believe these things were happening to me. The weekend had rolled around again, and it was party time. This time my brother and I were in bed.

When I woke to the goings on downstairs. People up and down the steps using the only bathroom in the house. I had the covers up to my face laying on my stomach. I could hear someone coming up the steps, as usual, to use the bathroom, but this time didn't go back downstairs, I could hear and sense that someone was standing in the door way to our room, then they walked into the room up to my bed and bumped my bed but, stood there for a moment.

Then touched me on my derriere. I moved my body away, then he moved his hand to touch himself. I could hear his labored breathing I was nervous since I didn't know why he was even in our room. I tried my best to fake sleep. Then he left and went back downstairs. I told myself the next chance I had to talk with my grandmother I'm going to tell her. Then I forgot about it. The following weekend came and the same thing, when it was time for us to come into the house.

I had the task of cleaning up the downstairs, this time while cleaning up, I found a wallet on my grandmother's couch, I tucked it under the couch pillow, and went to bed. When school rolled around that Monday, I took the money out of the wallet, and tucked it in my pockets and left the house. Took the cash to school, while sitting at the table with my classmates I pulled out the large wad of cash.

One kid got up and went to the teacher and told that I had a lot of money, flashing it. The teacher called me up to her desk, and told me to hand it over, and I gave it to her, sensing my hesitation that's when she said, all of it! She then gotten up and went to the Principals office.

They called my grandmother. I looked up and she was standing in the doorway to my classroom, telling me to come here, with her finger.

I rose from my seat, glancing over to my teacher, who didn't say a word, as I stepped out of class to see what my grandmother wanted. This was her first time since she enrolled me into school, that she had to come, and see about me. I knew soon as I saw her, that I was in big trouble! Soon as I approached her, she grabbed me by the scruff of my collar, and shoved me to the door leading out of the building.

Obviously angry, she said, through clenched teeth, where did you get this money from? She demanded. Scared to death, I told her, I found it, it was on the couch! She just kept repeatedly scuffing my shirt collar up all the way home, jerking me this way and that. Scaring me so bad, I peed my pants! We got inside of her house, she sent me upstairs to go take a bath, and I went to go run my bath water and got into the tub.

I listened for the steps, but didn't hear anything, so I relaxed, but just when I had forgotten all about what happened, she came up the steps, and burst through the bathroom door, and started whipping me with a switch, or in my case a tree branch without it's leaves. I tried to run and get out of the way, but there was no running and no hiding, I was stuck getting that whipping. I cried and screamed with every whack of the switch.

Until she got tired, then just as suddenly she appeared, she left. Days went by, when it was time to take the class silhouettes came, my grandmother hot combed and pressed my hair, she was really good at keeping my appearances up for school, anything that needed to be done, she didn't hesitate to make sure her granddaughter looked good, hair was done, and my clothes was neat

While she pressed my hair in preparation for the school's special day.

We talked, about everything, I openly told her that "Mr. Frank be touching me mama", she said he do? Where do he touch you at? For some reason I felt that she didn't believe me, like I had been making things up knowing my imagination knew no limits and perhaps my claims were just that, not true. I told her" different places, like on my bottom, there was another time he even tried to kiss me, but mama his mouth stink".

When she spoke, she remained calm," said" he does"? Well when do he do this"? I was gaining confidence now as I'm talking to her, I felt our close relationship was again in our grasp," I told her, it was one time while you were at work, or when you be sleep mama, when you be drinking, and you fall asleep, he come upstairs and come in my room, and touch my face, kiss on me and touch me between my legs mama, it hurt when he touch me down there.

But I tell him stop "I fell quiet after I had told her everything there was to tell. At least everything I had feared to tell her, up until now. My grandmother was quiet too, and didn't speak again, The next day I went to school, in class all of the students took turns choosing colored construction paper, then we lined up at the chalkboard, the teacher turned off the class lights, flipped the switch to the projector.

Each of us took turns standing in the light of the projector and the teacher carefully outlined each child's face onto the construction paper. Mine was blue. I took mine home to my grandmother, she hung it up for me. It wasn't long before I was outside playing. The weekend rolled around again, when we came in the house, the party was over, beer bottles everywhere in the living room, cups with liquor in them.

Sat strewn about all over the table, beer cans liquor bottles. I cleaned up the mess, I could hear my grandmother out front, talking, I imagined she must have been talking to Mr. Frank.

Silently I had hoped that she didn't tell him, what I had shared privately with her, after I finished cleaning, I quietly headed upstairs to bed. I climbed in and was falling asleep when I heard footsteps coming upstairs.

I climbed out of my bed and went and hid under the pile of clothes on the floor, in front of the closet, and put all the clothes on top of me. I was thinking if he can't find me, he will go away! He went into the bathroom, used the toilet, flushed it, waited a few minutes. Then came to the bedroom door, it was quiet, I didn't make a sound, then he walked into the room, then walked over to the pile on the floor.

Moving the clothes, and saw my foot, grabbed it and I kicked away at him, he asked in a hushed whisper "who's that"? and grabbed me, in one stroke scooped me up in his arm, and took me out the room, straight into my grandmother's bed, sat me down on the edge of her bed, shut the door behind him with one hand, unzipping his pants with the other hand. He grabbed my hand forcefully, in a hushed, gruff voice, said "touch it"

Pulling my hand roughly onto his private area, directing me how to touch him, this way and that I'd let my hand fall away, but immediately would grab my hand again, and guide me to touch him in a way that he liked, "yeah just like this, he whispered, slowly saying aw yeah, now I'm going to show you how to keep a man, he was beginning to gyrate his pelvis as if enjoying the moment, closer and closer to my mouth, then all of a sudden he stopped, and told me to wait a minute.

Then he opened the door, and walked to the toilet, went to go pee again. When I heard him urinating in the toilet, I jumped down off the bed, and ran to the window, I looked down, and saw my grandmother slumped to the side asleep in the lawn chair outside, sitting next to the 3 little steps that we had she was passed out! Behind me I could hear him come back into the bedroom.

When he opened the bedroom door, and saw me, while letting his pants fall to the floor, he just said," hey? what are you doing over there, walking towards me, said come back over here with me"? I didn't know what to do, I stood there frozen at the window, he walked over and grabbed me by the hand, and pulled me following him to the bed again, and sat me down, then he climbed in the bed and lay on his back, with me sitting beside him now, turned me to face his groin area, pulled out his member.

Put my hands on his partially erect penis, ordered me to stroke him more, shortly thereafter I heard movement, in the stairwell, but I sat quietly. Before he could utter his next words, the bedroom door swung wide open, the hallway light shining brightly inside, she was standing in the doorway, large and in charge saying Jackie? As if she had been looking for me for a long time, I sat there looking up at my grandmother.

I was relieved to see her, she had come to rescue me!, meanwhile he scooted off the side of the bed, and stood up. She only said" What's going on here"? My grandmother asked, I listened intently to her voice, she didn't sound drunk, I said" mama, he brought me in here"! They argued, and I ran downstairs, I heard my grandmother scream repeatedly get out!, get out!, get out of here!

Mr. Frank came running downstairs too, meanwhile arguing with my grandmother, all the way out the front door. My grandmother came downstairs, I could tell she was angry, but a little intoxicated too, she picked up the phone on the wall in the living room, when she saw me sitting there, dazed and confused. She yelled for me to go upstairs, so I went and climbed into my bed, pulled the covers up, and lay there in fear.

I could hear my aunt Gloria come into the house, in disbelief, raising her voice in response to what my grandmother was telling her, my aunt was saying" he did what"? "she did what" where is she at? I heard her running up the steps, straight into the room, Jackie!, "get up, get – up now right now!. Snatching the covers off me, I sat up in bed, rubbing my eyes, huh? I said, my aunt angrily saying to me, don't huh me! So, you having sex?

Confused I sat erect in bed and said huh? No! angrily she interrupted me, yes you are!, yanking me out of the bed, and began to physically beat me up with her fist, onto the bedroom floor, into the hallway, and all the way downstairs, about halfway she literally pulled me down the last 6 steps, by my hair, dragging me into the living room, punching me in the face and head.

I was screaming and crying the whole way.

When she got done beating me in the face and head, she was out of breath, heaving and in between breaths asked my grandmother what do you want to do with her? Mamma looked at me, and sadly said, I don't know what else to do. I looked up at her crying, my eyes begging for her not to give up on me!, please don't throw me away was all I could think, "mamma no!" in between cries, I begged and pleaded no!, my heart said don't do me like this.

I was so heart- broken all I could manage out of my mouth to my grandmother was no! I wanted desperately for her to save me from this night of horror, more and more it was looking like she gave up on me, threw me away to aunt glory. Then my aunt screamed at me, "Get in the closet!" I couldn't muster the strength to immediately jump up to her order, I lay there still crying, heaving from the blows.

I gotten up off the floor, and slowly moved toward the closet door, turned the door knob, still sniffling, and heaving. Looking at all the toys and clothes, I had shoved inside just days ago, I looked back to my beloved family members and whined," I can't, it's too much stuff", my aunt screamed" I don't care, get in there anyway", apparently so disgusted with me, they didn't want to look at me, finishing her statement," since you want to act like a dog, I'm going to treat you like one!"

I finally made my way into the closet, pushing aside coats, and toys to make room. Meanwhile upset crying, sniffling, heaving as I stood there. Then my aunt yelled" shut the door and shut up all that noise"! I tried my best to stand there quietly, waiting for my grandmother to finally get up and open the door. But every time I thought about earlier events and the whipping I just sustained I would cry again.

I could hear them somewhere between the living room and kitchen talking.

I was hoping my grandmother felt sorry for me. I stood there waiting, waiting, waiting, waiting. Hoping she would come open the door, mama please! I silently pleaded in my mind, please come get me, until I broke down crying again, pitiful tears of sorrow rained down my face while I peed my pants. I had stood for so long until I couldn't anymore.

In complete darkness I fumbled around until I could make a seat on the closet floor. I sat with my knees drawn to my chest, waiting for my grandmother. Waiting, waiting, waiting,, I fell asleep, the next time I woke up I heard footsteps coming down the steps, the little pitter patter was my little brother waking up and coming down stairs, just like we do every morning except he woke up to daylight, and I woke up to utter and complete darkness inside of a closet.

I did not move, out of my spot. I did sit there intently listening to my surroundings, I could hear him moving around out there, I heard my aunt mumbling something to him, and he remained quiet. Little did he know his big sister was held prisoner inside of the living room closet, in complete isolation, cut off from everything and everybody. Sometimes I would pretend I had company, that I was in school, I would see shapes and colors.

Bright and fluorescent colors vibrant all around me, this kept me entertained for a while, when I came back to my reality, It would sadden me all over again. I would hear my aunt glory interacting with my little brother from time to time, she would talk kind, loving, gentle to him, but to me it was as if she hated me, she was gruff, harsh and cold toward me. I couldn't help but wonder why?

A little while later I heard her voice, it was my grandmother, calling me out of the closet, I remember tentatively opening the door, then peeking around wondering if it really was her that called me, and not me hearing things or wishful thinking, Did I imagine her calling me? Slowly I opened the door, just in case I was wrong, I looked out and saw my grandmama! She was standing there just dialing the rotary phone to talk to someone.

She saw me, her eyes widened as if she hadn't seen me in a long time, surprised at what she was looking at she asked me, " What happened to your face, why are you so swollen"? I shrugged my shoulders, as if to say I don't know, walking up to her slowly, not caring in the least how I looked, I just wanted badly to hug my mama, I desperately needed a hug after all this time, walked up with my arms outstretched for a hug.

Whomever she was waiting to talk to came on the line her conversation became far more important. I dropped my arms, and stood by her and quietly waited, when she looked up to see me looking at her, she nonchalantly turned her back to me, when she got ready she turned to me, told me" go on upstairs and take a bath!" I walked away and made my way upstairs into the bathroom.

Ran my bathwater, took off my underwear and stepped into the tub. I couldn't help but notice how light looks so different when you don't have sight. I sat in the water for a long time, my feet were wrinkled when I finally gotten out of the tub, I went into my room, and searched for a shirt and some pants to put on. I climbed into my bed and I lay there until I was called downstairs, when I came down.

My aunt Glory was just sitting there in the kitchen, but facing the living room, my grandmother must have stepped out. When she saw me, she ordered me to sit on the couch, I sat down as I was told, she just sat there looking at me for a while before she spoke, then blurted out to me you are one ugly, little girl, do you know that? I don't know how anybody can stand to look at you, with those big bubble lips!

They are big enough to cover your whole face. That's the only reason those little boys like you because all they can see on you are those big lips of yours. I quietly sat there, I looked at her periodically, but I would also look away, from time to time I would imagine really big lips on my face, I stayed quiet not saying a word, because the memory of her beating me to a pulp, and inflicting pain is still fresh in my mind.

Still I was confused and wondered why was she saying those mean things to me,? Then I remembered Mr. Frank and figured that was why because of him, then I assumed it was my fault that he did things to me. I sat totally still while she hailed assaults at me, one after another I had no other choice but to take it, never once did I respond back to her. Although it hurt whenever she spewed each word to me.

I wanted to get up and leave, but again out of fear of another altercation with her, I sat perfectly still. Eventually I started envisioning me with gigantic lips on my face, huge nose with absolutely no room for my eyes. I envisioned a mass of ugliness for myself. She asked me, did I want to come live with her, it took a second for me to say no, but I thought better of it, stone faced I sat and just shook my head up and down in a yes motion.

Somebody knocked on the door, then opened it, as I looked I saw my uncle Paul walk through the door. He and my aunt sat in the kitchen and talked among themselves, then my grandmother walked in the door shortly thereafter, then all 3 sat at the kitchen table talking. I continued to sit on the couch, where I was instructed earlier to sit by my aunt. When they ended their family meeting, my uncle Paul stood up and called me into the kitchen.

Chapter 5

They all announced that I would be staying with them for a little while, I immediately thought about my little cousin their daughter Tammy who was about my age, and welcomed the opportunity, I looked at my grandmother expecting a hug goodbye or confirmation, but instead she sat stone faced in the chair, and watched as we left her home. When we stepped outside I looked around for my little brother, but I didn't see him, so I followed my uncle to his car.

Up until now, I had only seen my uncle with his car, he was always tinkering with it for one reason or the other, but today I actually was getting the chance to ride in it with him. I sat in the front seat beside my uncle, watching him as he drove through the streets, neither one of us saying a word, quietly I sat listening to the music he played on his radio.

He broke the silence by saying" so you know what sex is now huh? I fell quiet again after that, because I didn't know what he was talking about. I felt most comfortable talking about school. He pulled into the parking spot, in front of the apartment building and turned off the engine, and I followed his lead, when he opened his door, I too opened mine, and I stood looking around, I had never seen this area before.

I followed him up the steps into the building, he closed the door behind me, and led the way up the stairs, to the apartment where he lived, which was off E. North Ave, near

E. Greenmount, across from The Administration Building, and Baltimore Parole and Probation. They lived on the third floor, we came to the second floor, walked through the hallway, passed two apartments along the way, to the third- floor landing.

Their apartment was the very first one at the top of the stairwell. I waited as he put his key in the door and opened it, inside was his live- in girlfriend Lilly, her daughter Tammy, and new baby Taylor. The apartment was rather dark inside, with the bedroom shades drawn. The kitchen however was a tad bit brighter in comparison, because the light was on. The tv was going and my cousin Tammy was sitting at the table watching it.

Lilly was in the bedroom watching over her newborn son. She did get up however when she heard the door, and saw my uncle come inside with me behind him, I said hello to everybody, and my uncle told me to take a seat in the kitchen, while he talked with her inside the bedroom. I sat in the kitchen at the table with my cousin as she watched tv. I looked around the kitchen and taking in the view.

It was a tiny one bedroom apartment, coming in the front door was the kitchen, painted in antique white paint, a pantry with a door, cabinet on the wall, then an apartment sized stove, the window with a fire escape attached, then beside the window was the sink, then another cabinet for the dishes, then the kitchen table with three chairs, the tv sat against the wall on the table, then the wall gave way to the bedroom, inside the bedroom was a window.

A full-sized bed, and a twin bed for Tammy, then the bathroom, next to the bathroom was the front door. My uncle left back out of the apartment, and I sat there with Tammy, watching tv. for a while, when my uncle came back he brought dinner, for everybody to eat, chicken and French fries and biscuits, then afterward it was time for us to go to bed, I shared the bed with Tammy, she slept at the top and I at the bottom of the bed.

The next day when I woke up, my uncle had already left for work. Now, it was just the females left in the house. The first thing I did when I woke up was use the bathroom, went to go sit at the table and watch tv. I pulled up a chair and sat next to her, all day each day. My favorite show was Captain Chesapeake, I liked other cartoons as well, but he was my favorite. Sometimes Tammy and I would disagree.

Mostly on who was who and who did what, and what to watch next. I had gotten used to the idea of watching whatever came on. Naturally I would soon get bored and I would look for other things to do to occupy my time. I looked around for a toy, as soon as I became occupied with a toy, or show any interest in it, Tammy would yell" That's mine! Give it back!" I would hand it over just to keep her quiet.

I sat there bored until Lilly decided to cook, she would come into the kitchen and put together a good meal, sometimes Lilly would make us go into the other room, while she cooked.

We sat quietly and played together, then she would call out to us, to go and wash our hands and get ready for dinner. Tammy and I would race to the bathroom, to beat each other to the kitchen table before the other got there.

We would pull up to the table and eat as ravenously as two little girls could. Some days I would sing, clap and dance, I repeated everything I learned to do when I went to school, and shared what all I remembered with my cousin, I had to learn to be quiet because the baby would be asleep. I remember one day sitting at the table, my aunt Lilly had just finished combing and brushing Tammy's hair, into cute little ponytails.

Complete with colorful hair balls in different colors, and various shapes. A style I wasn't used to seeing, and I liked it a lot, as Tammy watched tv, I played in her hair, picking them each up and looking at them, she whined for me to leave her alone. I had gotten yelled at that day for bothering her, my feelings were a little hurt, and I didn't bother with her anymore after that.

A week or two went by.

I had left shreds of toilet paper on the floor. I had gotten yelled at and was told that my uncle will know about it when he gets home from work! This made me a little nervous, because I didn't know if he would be upset, or not. I had some anxiety as a result. We were watching tv, and I had forgotten all about earlier incident, when we heard the key in the door, then he emerged.

I looked at him as he walked in the door, he didn't say anything to anybody, he went straight into the bedroom to Lilly, they sat and talked, I couldn't hear what they were saying because the tv was going at the same time. I could hear him go into the bathroom, he must have seen the mess, and when he came back out, he called me, "Jackie, come here" I quietly rose from my seat and went to him, which he was standing at the bathroom doorway, huh?

I responded, and he asked me directly, "why did you leave that paper on the floor like that"?

I looked up at him like a deer caught in headlights, wide-eyed and nervous, not knowing what to expect, and shrugged my shoulders quietly looking at the ground," you don't know"? he asked with more authority in his voice, talking to me while simultaneously taking off his belt from around his waist,

I guess we are going to find out in a minute wont we?" and lifted the belt, high in the air and came down with a whack against the back of my legs, and backside as I turned to run, but he just kept on whacking. I cried out as it landed time after time on my arm, my shoulder, my neck and ear. Then I ran away from him, and faced him on the other side of the bed crying, loudly, angrily he said where you going?

I'm not done with you! Lilly sat in the corner out of the way, I saw her as I was looking around franticly to find a place to run to, as he approached me to finish beating on me some more. I'd gotten down on the floor, and quickly crawled under the twin bed, to get away from him and the belt, when he saw what I had done, he called for me to come out, but I didn't move. He said Jackie" If you don't come out, its going be worse when I get you"!

Still crying no, no! it did allow me some time for the pain to start going away. He was reaching under the bed, but I kept moving, that's when the whole bed came up, I had stood up, but because he was standing in the way I couldn't get around him into the kitchen, so I was stuck in the bed room, he put the bed down, and grabbed me by the arm and shoved me into the kitchen, While walking away.

I could hear him say and I better not hear a peep out of you no more tonight or I'm coming in there, still upset but not crying profusely like I was, I took my seat. My cousin never stopped watching tv the whole time, she looked at me for a split second and that was it. She went back to watching tv. I sat for as long as I could, but pretty soon I was sleepy, I crossed my arms and laid my head down just like we did in school.

My uncle ate and took his bath, after that we girls went to bed. It didn't take me long to figure out that my cousin and I were totally different kids, she didn't interact much, in fact I didn't notice one time that she ever played with any toys, or barbie dolls, a ball or any other toy for that matter, nor did she talk much either, she was far quieter than I. In fact, she seemed more distant now that I currently live with them.

Far more stoic than I remember, no longer the lively, playful little girl that used to come over to my grandmother's house. If I dare say it, she seemed unnatural, and zombie like, she wasn't fun to be around like I had previously thought. Back when they visited, I would often imagine that life was happy, perfect for them as a family. Something that I desired deep down in my gut from time to time.

I would inquire of my grandmother about my biological father. Since I knew my mother and wasn't too thrilled with the memories I had of her, somehow I had convinced myself that if my mother was a bad person, then my father surely must have been good, which made me want to see and meet him all the more. But as it stands, in reality this little girl had what I didn't, yet she seemed more distant, like things had changed between us.

As if I had done something wrong to her that made her change her mind about being friends with me. I on the other hand was a busy body, curious about everything in my surroundings, very impulsive and subject to dream, and live out fantasies. Always exploring, looking for the next adventure. Needing challenge for mental growth and maturity. Living with my uncle was boring for me.

Of course back then, I was intellectually incapable of conveying that to them in a way they could comprehend and allow them time to meet my needs. Naturally for me, I would do things to combat boredom, being in that tiny pintsized apartment, unable to go anywhere or do anything constructive was damaging. Nothing to do but sit at the kitchen table and watch tv all day. I would sit and stare at the kitchen walls.

I can recall a extralarge dark wooden fork and spoon hanging on the nails in the wall there was a clock too. Every so often after watching so much tv, for so very long, I would stare at the fork and spoon, to just give my eye a break from the 13" tv all day every day from the moment we wake up in the morning. Until the moment my aunt announced it was time to go to sleep. The kitchen was our playroom, so to speak.

Except we weren't allowed to do anything except watch tv. I don't even recall hearing the baby cry much at all come to think of it. I would imagine my aunt could have been a little bored too, because she sat in the bedroom all day in the corner by the window. Weeks came and went when the time came when my uncle decided to trust me to go to the corner store to purchase small items for them.

I remember the stern talk my aunt gave me before sending me off to the store, she said" Don't you lose this money, this is our last" then she gave me the directions how to get there and back again, Ok I would say, and head out the door. I took the money with a note, held it tightly in my hand then take the exact route my aunt sent me. It was a corner store ran by the Jamaicans, the music played in the background when you walked in.

I walked into the store and handed the man my crumbled money and note, I stood eyeballing all the ice cream wrappers on the wall, indicating which flavors were available, they took up the whole wall. He said a few words to his employees, then he came back with a brown bag, I reached up to the turnstile and took the bag with the items and left, walked back to the apartment, walked up the steps and knocked on the door.

Aunt Lilly opened the door, she said "good!" now go back and sit down, I asked, kind of whining could I go back outside, please? but she told me no, so I went back to the kitchen and took my seat. Nothing more to do than to sit and watch tv the rest of the day away. When it was time to eat, I had an appetite, I would eat my food, and would look for seconds, if my cousin left anything I wanted I would eat hers too.

Later my uncle Paul would get in from work. I saw him as the stern disciplinarian, his girlfriend was stern too but not as much, she was the home body, he was the brawny tough work hard all day, come home be with his family, eat, sleep and sometimes take a bath. We knew it was bedtime for us, it was a standard that we could set our internal clocks to. I didn't have any problems with falling asleep, it came quick for me.

Generally as soon as my body laid down, I would be fast asleep, slept through the night. The next day came, I had gotten up did my usual, in the bathroom, then head straight for the kitchen, at some point through the day, my aunt called me into the bedroom, I immediately gotten up to go see whatever it is that she wanted, as I was instructed to do by my uncle, when I arrived, she said to me " I need you to go to the store, here take this note, don't you lose this, because it's our last little bit ok?"

Ok I agreed, and headed out the door, the only time I could feel like I'm a big girl, I took my time going down the steps, I wanted to take in as much as I could, enjoy as much freedom as possible. Knowing I would be on lock down for the rest of the day, until the next time she has a need, by the time I made it outside some of the neighborhood kids were out there, quietly I blended right in with them as they walked up the street.

By the time we all made it up to the top of the block, my mind went blank and I started playing with them, they were equipped with baseball bat, and ball, I merged in with them, running to catch the ball, throwing it back, yelling for the ball, and waiting my turn to swing the bat, and hit the ball as far as

I could, and watch the boys run and retrieve it. I was having a really good time. Woohoo! I was free, in my comfort zone.

I was in my element ripping and running, to me it was what I was born to do, and boy I could run like the wind, I was swift, darting in and out, this way and that just to get under the ball, in a prime position to catch it. It wasn't until the whole game started to slow down that the thought occurred to me, what I initially was supposed to be doing, why I was even outside in the first place!

I looked up to see the store in view and headed towards it, I ran inside, full well knowing time was ticking, and I needed to get back. Headed straight for the counter as I had done so many times before. Sweaty and dirty from playing. Standing there, the man asked me" what do you want"? I went to hand him the note my aunt had given me earlier, oops! I came up empty, "wait" I said, looking around.

Checking my pockets, nothing, empty again, looking around on the floor, nothing! I hurried to the door, surely I must have dropped it, back down the street head down to the ground, eyes searching, this way and that I went looking and still nothing. Oh no! I started to think to myself, I must have dropped it somewhere, but where? Somewhere at some point I knew I had to go back home.

It's looking like I'm going to be empty handed, because I couldn't find the crumbled piece of paper and money she had given me! I yelled to the kids, if they saw anything on the ground, but they all just looked up, but kept on playing. My heart was sinking, and fear was creeping in at the mere thought of going back, showing up empty handed. I kept looking, searching heading back to my uncle's place.

The closer I got to his place, the stark reality of my situation was playing out in my head, thinking and imagining how mad my aunt is going to be, if and when I walk in the door without the stuff she sent me for. I could see her face, in my imagination angrily yelling at me, I kept my eyes to the ground looking around diligently, persistently. I knew in my heart that I had dropped the wad of note and money.

But to no avail, before I knew it I was back at the steps of the apartment, heading back upstairs, I knocked on the door, tammy answered, and opened the door, I walked inside, feeling lost, depleted, tired because I searched with all my might and still came up empty. I walked slowly into the bedroom, straight to my aunt, she looked at me, asked "Where, is the stuff, I sent you for"?

With a commanding tone, full of expectancy, my head lowered, my eyes swelling with tears but not saying a word, just shrugged my shoulders. That not being enough for her simply said, " Huh? She raised her voice loudly, as if saying to me speak up! Suddenly jarring me out of my head space, quietly, sheepishly I mustered" I, I don't know" as truthful as I knew how. My voice cracking under the pressure. If she only knew how difficult it was for me already.

It was nightmarish to have to tell her, although it was my truth, I really did not know what happened to it, one minute I was leaving out the apartment door with a feeling of complete intentions, full of direction and focus, the next minute my mind went completely blank. When I reached outside, it was like I had totally and completely forgotten everything. There was, a dark space, empty and void.

I saw the other kids, being kids and I completely lost it (excuse the pun) WHAT? She yelled!

"You mean to tell me! you lost my money!" she stormed, She was angry, no! she was furious, she said to me, "Girl! GET OUT

OF MY FACE LITTLE GIRL!" her tone dripping with venom, her face was distorted, lips pursed. I could feel that she was ready to rip me apart. Crushed, I walked away.

Saddened by the way I felt, and what I just did to this family. I felt a tremendous and heavy burden on my countenance, I felt like a complete and utter failure. As she went on and on about it, my thoughts were no longer my own, as I listened to her even while I headed to the kitchen, my head hung low. I couldn't feel my feet anymore, was I walking or drifting now? Even into the kitchen I could still hear her.

"you just wait, until your uncle gets home"! she'd threaten, interrupting my flow and thought pattern, my eyes widened, fear crept back in, No! I yelled out, knowing he would be angry with me, I burst into tears. I knew when I was outside that things were going to get ugly. I sat down in my seat angrily plop! Angrily folding my arms, tears streaming down my face. Quietly as the day ebbed onward my fear and anger subsided.

Watching tv with my cousin who didn't say a word, nor cared to talk to me. I laughed at what I thought was funny in the cartoons, time had crept slowly by before I heard the key in the door, I looked at the door, my heart sinking to my feet! He stepped inside and looked into the kitchen at us, headed straight into the bedroom to his girlfriend and baby. They were quietly talking, as I watched tv.

Half listening to it now, but when I looked up again, he was standing in the doorway to the bedroom, looking dead at me, anger in his eyes, meanwhile taking off his belt, "come here!" he said to me, walking toward me, with the belt raised in the air, in my seat I recoiled, with my hands raised to catch the blow coming. "Nooo!" I began to scream, eyeballing the raised belt coming at me," you lost my money"?

More of a statement, than a question, whack, whack, whack! with the leather belt across my arms, head, face, shoulder, "Ouch"! I screamed, arms flailing about trying to block the assault and tried to get up and run, but I was ambushed and cornered in the chair, whacking me across my head and back, he would push me back down up against the sink into my seat, my cousin tammy gotten up and ran into the room with her mother.

It was just I and my uncle now, with my arms still trying my best to block the pings and stings of the belt, we were knocking stuff over in the kitchen, chairs flying this way and that, I was backing up into the stove, with him grabbing my limbs and whacking away. Somehow I was being pinned on the floor under the weight of his knee, whipping me. I would never just lay there and take a beating.

I would always try to catch the blows of the belt in my hands rather than on my flesh. It was more like a fight between uncle and niece, while he would struggle to get a good shot at me with the belt, to make his statement. By the time he was finished, he was heaving heavily and sweat pouring from his forehead. I scooted myself backward and away from him into the corner of the kitchen on the other side of the stove, he angrily glaring at me, as he walked past me into the bedroom to his girlfriend, and little girl.

Then came back into the kitchen, and ordered me to "get up!" like a drill sergeant, and led me to the window, still breathing heavy, angrily told me to "get out there!', I quietly did as I was told, not knowing what his plan was, but in my mind it was better than being beat up again. When I climbed out, I stood up on the fire escape, and walked a little ways and was about to sit down on the steps leading downstairs.

He stopped me short of sitting down, barked a command. "No! over here!" pointing to the spot directly in front of the apartment window then lowering his voice. Sensing he was angry, I walked back to the window, and sat down in the spot he directed me to, I sat Indian styled on the fire escape, he looked at me intently and said, "Now sit here, until I decide what to do with you"! then he turned and walked away from the window.

Angrily I put my face in my hand, with elbows into my crossed legs. I watched him from the fire escape move through the kitchen, realigning the table, erecting the chairs back up to the table again. Fixing the tv in just the right spot, and then disappear into the bedroom with his family.

Chapter 6

A little while later, as I sat on the fire escape looking around, I started to take notice of the trees that grew so very tall, even past the fire escape.

Stopping just short of reaching the roof of the building. I watched as my aunt Lilly came into the kitchen, start to put together a meal for her family. She never did utter a word to me, in fact she never even looked my way, to at least acknowledge me sitting there looking at her, while she went about her duty. As I observed her moving around inside, washing this dish, and that pot, the fragrance of what she was preparing began wafting in the summer breeze.

Through the window where I sat, I fidgeted in my seat, smelling the cooking of fried chicken, macaroni & cheese. The sun was now gone to bed, there I sat there on the fire escape, in the dark, except for the beam of light emanating through the kitchen window, trying my best to be a good girl, so they would let me come back inside and be a part of the family atmosphere again.

My uncle and his little girl walked into the kitchen.

When dinner was ready, and they all 3 sat down at the table to eat, the first I had ever witnessed, since living there with them. Patiently I waited, waited and quietly waited, listening as they talked among themselves, not looking in my direction. I called out, from time to time, in case they'd forgotten about me. Never looking at me, nor responding. They finally finished eating, it wasn't until later that my aunt came back in, made a plate then sat it on the table, disappeared into the bedroom.

My uncle showed up, told me to come inside, stood aside as I climbed back into the kitchen, ordered me to eat, then escorted me to bed. The next day I woke up, my cousin was already in her favorite seat, quietly watching tv. I went to the bathroom, thinking everything was back to normal. I walked into the kitchen and took my seat, soon as she heard me pull the chair out, and take my seat at the table, my aunt called out.

"Hey! What did your uncle tell you, get back out there"! I got up and climbed through the window and angrily took my seat on the iron fire escape. It was early and the sun was just beginning to increase its heat, all day I sat, from sun-up. to sun-down. Sometimes I would dream about walking off and never coming back, just walking down the steps, into my play world, where it was expected for children to play.

Have fun for as long as I wanted. Staring at the brick walls on the backside of the apartment building, from the fire escape was not my idea of fun. There was a knock at the door, my aunt Lilly answered the door, then came to the window and told me to go downstairs, to my other aunt's house. I had to climb back into the house, open the door and go down the steps, when I reached the 2nd landing.

The apartment door was wide open, I went inside, it was huge! A whole lot bigger than upstairs. In fact if I had to make an comparison, I would say my aunt's apartment make my uncle's place look like a sardine can, everybody is packed inside of his place, plus they keep it rather dark inside, reminiscent of a funeral parlor with all the curtains drawn, and no lights on, except at night the kitchen, bathroom.

I stood quietly taking in the surroundings, and how bright her place was, in contrast. My aunt was in the kitchen cooking dinner, and apparently had not seen me in a long time, wanted to see how much I had grown. The last time I saw her was at my grandmother's place, but that all seemed so long ago now. I walked from the door through the living room into the kitchen where she was preparing her meal I just stood there.

Looking around I could see that her bedroom was a small portion of the living room, she had a large table and mirror with all her hair accessories on it. After saying hello to my aunt, I walked around taking in the atmosphere, when I came to the table, I saw scissors and picked them up, staring into the mirror at myself, decided I was ugly and quietly, not saying a word, in one clip cut the whole patch of hair off my widow's peak.

My cousin Angela saw me, ran over and immediately grabbed my hand and took the scissors from me, called to her mother, who told her to escort me back upstairs. To what I call nightmare. The very place I didn't want to be. For the first time, since my uncle came and picked me up from my grandmother's, I saw myself, I was unkept, my clothes were ragged, filthy from old food droppings.

Clothes unwashed, no one combed nor brushed my hair, my uncle is treating me less than human, I can't go outside to play with other kids, I can't socialize with anyone, my age or otherwise. I was saddened but didn't know it. These things I dare not say to my family members face to face, so out of fear I would keep all my feelings inside. No one never said to me that it was ok to openly say whatever it is on my mind.

Instead however, whenever I talked or played I was always told to shut up! be quiet, stop that! don't do this, don't do that! totally reinforcing the idea in my head that my input was not valuable, I was not validated, not honored, not respected. So, would somebody please tell me what can I do? As a child not having the capacity to convey feelings out of fear of retaliation from an adult.

Experiences intense feelings but ultimately learns to suppress them just to be able to cope, or function, thus avoiding less than ideal behaviors or reactions from the adult. Once back inside the apartment, I was ordered by my aunt Lilly to take my seat back outside on the fire escape. The only time I was allowed back inside, was to use the bathroom, and to eat, that's it. I sat there like I was told.

When I got ready I would call aunt Lilly to request to use the bathroom, "Go ahead" she would say so I would climb back in, sauntered past my cousin Tammy, taking my time to the bathroom, once inside I would drink water from the sink's faucet or tub, pee, but afterward I would sit on the toilet and just swing my feet, entertaining myself as best as I could with the toilet paper. With absolutely nothing to do on the fire escape.

Everything else looked more interesting, entertaining when I finished, I came out, and looked at my aunt Lilly who was sitting upright in the chair, watching her baby sleep, I made my way into the kitchen, carefully taking notice of what was on the tv. since I couldn't see it from the window, especially through the glare of the sun's rays. Tammy continued to watch tv. and I did too, forgetting the fact that I was supposed to be taking my seat on the fire escape.

Enough time had elapsed, my aunt Lilly walked to the bathroom, then came back out, then walked into the kitchen, saw me standing there, nastily warned me saying" your uncle is on his way home, you better get back outside where you belong!" I climbed back out the window, and took my seat, I sat quietly and watched as aunt Lilly made preparations to start cooking her meal, for her family.

She talked to her little girl from time to time, but not to me, soon I would start smelling her food as it perked up and simmered the herbs and seasoning that peppered her food, from where I sat, I would catch a good whiff of what she was cooking, and it smelled good, then the door would open, and in popped my uncle, he spoke to my aunt and they both walked into the bedroom. It was like watching them on tv, from my seat.

Meanwhile my bottom was bothering me sitting on hot metal, all day long was very uncomfortable, so I stood up and started walking around I also sat on the steps, I walked around again, trying to entertain myself, I sat down again in front of the window, I yelled out" can I use the bathroom?" but it really was a chance to stretch my legs, and to douse my face with some cold water.

I walked to the bathroom, forgetting the fact that my uncle was now home, I didn't even bother to look for him, I went into the bathroom and shut the door, and proceeded to busy myself after I wiped, myself with the toilet paper, I would sit on the toilet and shred it, bit by tiny bit, by the time I finished there were tiny pieces on the floor, sink and tub. I had not even taken notice I just left the bathroom and walked into the kitchen and climbed back out the window.

Dinner was ready and they all sat down to eat, just as they had many nights ago, it was shaping up to be their new normal, all I could do was sit there and watch I wanted to come in, but the fear of another physical altercation was looming in my mind, they finished eating and then got up and went into the bedroom. It was a long while before my aunt came back and made another plate for me.

So long in fact I had started to get agitated and worried that they somehow wouldn't feed me, but soon as I was beginning to imagine the worse, she appeared, and put a plate of food on the table, then walked out, yelling behind her as she rounded the corner" Go ahead and eat!" I got up and climbed down from the window, and pulled out a chair, sat down and dug into my food, just when I was about to shove the second spoonful into my mouth.

My uncle appeared with his belt in hand, "Get up!" he ordered as I looked up, he was headed straight for me again with belt raised above his head, I immediately started yelling & screaming as I raised my arms in defense to block the belt as much as I could, in the midst of him whacking away at me, he reminded me of the toilet paper, telling me how disobedient I am, how hard headed I am, and that I don't listen, by this time I was up on my feet.

Cornered between the table and refrigerator, every time he hit me with the belt I would use my hands to try and block the landing on my legs and torso, suddenly, abruptly he stopped to go inside the bathroom and run the bathwater, I stood in the kitchen rocking from one foot to the other, crying in a heated, feverish pitch repeatedly pleading saying no, no! He just loudly threatened me that the belt would hurt 5x's more.

With this hot steaming water on it, sitting on the edge of the tub, running the water on the belt, every so often folding it, and snapping it to strengthen the belt, thus making it's impact more pronounced upon my skin, I was jumping up & down out of frustration, shaking and wringing my hands, I could not believe that he would think to do something like this to me! In my mind how could he be so cruel to me, to want to hurt me like this?

I would come to the kitchens' doorway, to peer into the bathroom, then duck back out of his sight, and crying more loudly upon seeing that he was serious with his threat. After sinking and thoroughly saturating the belt, he would stretch and snap his belt, by folding it length wise from tip to end, bunch the belt in the middle then quickly pull it outward making a snapping sound, every time he did that, I thought to myself,

"Oh no! I am going to get the whipping of a lifetime, now!" When he was done, he proceeded to get up and come toward me with his belt in hand, I was screaming crying no! with my arms extended in the air to block the whacks, I was backing up into the kitchen wall, with nowhere else to go, he rained down whack after whack, the belt upon my hands, arms, my head, my back, everywhere I turned I would get hit.

I just kept reaching upward until I felt something, I grabbed it as he was hitting me continuously, what I was holding in my hand broke in shards as he was whacking away, I just held onto the wood decoration toward his face, every time he hit me, my body would jerk poking him in the process. He was so enraged that he did not see me grab the wooden fork off the wall, chunks would break off as it would wildly strike the table.

Until in my anger each time he hit me with the belt, I would swing the fork striking him right back with it, whack for whack, he finally stopped whipping me when he realized something was wrong! He noticed he wasn't the only one standing there with a weapon! He quietly observed that I had struck him multiple times, because he was now bleeding, his eyes widened as he grabbed his wound on the side of his face.

Sharply turned and stormed into the bathroom, then slammed the door shut. I stood there, motionless not sure what just happened, he left me standing in the kitchen with the what was left of the wooden fork in my hand, the whole house was eerily quiet, when I heard my aunt Lilly call out for me to go to bed! Dropping my weapon, I quietly walked into the bedroom, slipped into the bed and quickly fell off to sleep.

The next day I had woke up to use the bathroom, afterward I joined my cousin at the kitchen table to watch tv. as I sat there I had a weird feeling in my gut that something is about to happen, but I disregarded it and continued watching tv. I remembered the night before, as I watched tv, I kept getting vivid pictures seeing my uncle bleeding. I then thought maybe he would come after me again, like they do on tv, to seek revenge or something.

As I sat I privately hoped that my aunt Lilly would not make me go and sit back on the fire escape again, I actually hoped that she had forgotten. I grew to dislike sitting out on the fire escape, all day long, I learned to lie, would fake having to use the bathroom, luckily it was the middle of the summer, and not the winter where I probably would have frozen to death. It hadn't rained much, but it was unbearably hot outside.

Sitting on that hot metal fire escape all day long, it wasn't until after my uncle would get home from work and eat with his family, would I finally not only allowed to eat the one and only meal of the day, but also be allowed to sit on a different surface other than that hot metal, like a wooden chair at the kitchen table, no water all day, except for when I went to the bathroom, I would drink from the face bowl, or the tub.

Perhaps I wasn't neat enough with the water preventing it from getting on the floor. When I heard the key in the door I knew it would be my uncle, but what I didn't know is that he would tell me to come and go with him. Happily I rose from my seat and never looked back, I followed him out the door, down the stairs, I glanced over at my other aunt's door, it looked just as before, when I first saw it, like nobody lived there.

We kept going down the stairs and out to the car. I stood at the car door not knowing what to do, he proceeded to walk around to the driver's side, told me to get in and we both piled in. He started the car and it roared and then settled down to a purr, he didn't even look at me, or joke with me like he used to do before I came to live with them. He put the car into drive, then pulled out into the street and we were on our way.

The drive was quiet, nobody said a word, I just kept looking out at the street as we passed houses, stores and everything in between. Soon we were pulling up in front of my grandmother's house. I saw kids running this way and that, I opened my door and walked behind my uncle up to my grandmother's door, he turned the knob and walked in. My Grandmother was home, sitting in the kitchen.

She smiled as we walked in. I stood there as they talked, then he left, didn't say anything to me, nor I to him. My grandmother asked" are you hungry"? Yes mam I would respond, she told me" go on upstairs and clean yourself up, she said with an air of disgust, and after you eat I've got to do something with that head of yours!" yes mam I responded, and went on up the steps, went into the bathroom and ran my bathwater then I climbed in.

I sat there then washing myself. When I was done I went into the bedroom and found my clothes, and finally put on some clean clothes! Everything seemed so long ago, even though nothing has changed at home. I went back downstairs, as I walked up I saw she had a plate ready for me, she asked me" are you ok"? I nodded my head saying "yes mam" as I approached the table to take a seat,

I felt a twinge of pain that I couldn't identify with as I took my first bite of food, mashed potatoes, chicken and spinach. My grandmother stood back and quietly watched me eat, probably contemplating what my uncle had told her about me, as I ate I asked "where was my little brother"?, she just said "oh he's outside playing, you can go on out there when your done eating, I'm going upstairs" yes mam I said.

I caught up with him later, I couldn't believe how he had grown, he was taller than I remembered, but still it was great to be back home. He asked me where have you been? I told him "had to stay with Uncle Paul for a little while" he just said oh!, I thought I wasn't going to see you anymore"! I told him you still ugly, he said you too! we laughed and went on in the house and headed up to bed.

The next day my grandmother left for work, and we were home alone and we played each having their own space and toys, eventually I wandered into my grandmother's room, I casually start looking through her stuff, my little brother found me and came in too, and joined me in looking around, she had a closet just like the one we had in our room, walk in closet, she had all kinds of books on the shelf.

CHAPTER 7

Different colored shoe boxes and other things, stuff I hadn't noticed before, so I had gotten a chair and stood up and gathered a few of the boxes and put them on the table, we curiously started looking through them, my brother opened a box while I was busy looking in another and found a gun, I hadn't noticed at first as his back was turned to me, I just happened to look up and he was waving and mock aiming a gun!

In shock, I said "ooh what's that?" with his big wide grin, saying "I'm John Wayne" brandishing the gun, Give it to me! I raised my voice, and snatched it out of his hand, he went to snatch it back but wasn't quick enough, nor tall enough as I held it above his head, and placed it high up on the shelf out of his reach. Then went back to nosing around, after the boxes I looked under the bed, then lifted the mattress,

Saw a single item, something white, a cylinder or long white tube made of thin metal. It had a metal cap on it, I grabbed it, and let the mattress fall, as we inspected the casing. We opened the tube and found it was full of dimes. I slid some out onto my hand to make sure, and it was confirmed. I grabbed one dime and put the rest back, then I announced to my little brother that I'm going to the store,

I will be right back. I left out the back door and headed down the walkway across the other court onto Westview St. and down to the corner store, I walked in and saw all the ice cream wrappings neatly taped on the wall, all the candy jugs neatly showcasing the multiple assorted flavors. Candy then was only a penny a piece, which allowed me to get a whole lot of goodies for my brother and I.

Headed back home with my candy to share with him as we played the rest of the day away, and also watched cartoons until my grandmother came home from work. She came in took a seat in the living room kicking off her shoes and asked us, "so? What did you two do all day?" I went first, I told her that Justice and I played make pretend all day, she just looked at me, nodding her head "you did huh"?

Yes, mam I said, then she looked at Justice, asked him, "what did you all do today"? First Justice told her about the gun we had found in her room, then he told her about the dimes that I had found under her mattress, and that I had went to the store and brought candy. I shot my little brother the look of dread, I could not believe he had shamelessly told her everything I had done. "No! I didn't,"

I lied in protest, "Yes you did" he retorted! Loud and strong, I fell quiet as I realized the jig was up. My grandmother just smiled a pleasing smile toward her grandson, as he did not disappoint, but looked at me with pity, saying, a lot has changed since you been gone, she had said it with an air of pride in her grandson, but to me as if she had arranged for him to tell her everything that I do, like she had groomed him.

Trained him, nurtured him, to be her tattle tale on the big sister. I folded my arms in disdain and defiance. My grandmother demanded that I stand in the corner, until she went upstairs. I did as I was told and stood in the corner. When she got ready, she went upstairs, as she climbed closer to the top of the landing, my heart began to sink, as I recalled the mess we made earlier, "uh oh" I thought to myself.

"I'm in for it now!, I'm about to get a whipping of my life. As she entered the room, she silently took in the scene and mess, I could hear her every move up-stairs, she looked into our room, then after a minute she went into her room, she was quiet for a long time, I stood there wondering what to do, what was about to happen? Still I stood there, the longer she waited upstairs, the more I was filled with anxiety as to what my outcome would be.

Finally I heard her footsteps coming back down toward the bottom step, I heard her exhale in her weary and tired, as if to say " I just don't know what else to do with you!" exasperated kind of way. As she rounded the corner to the living room, I saw her face, such pain and confusion, I could see that she was mentally struggling, trying to figure out what to do next. As I watched her take her seat on the couch.

I felt shame, and regret, at the pain and discomfort that I was putting my beloved grandmother through. She said nothing, but I could tell the softness in her face was gone, replaced by tense frown lines and worry. I couldn't take it anymore, the quiet, suspense was choking me, I couldn't take her being angry with me, I really would much rather die, than to have her feeling negatively towards me!

I broke the silence, with my head hung low in a broken and contrite position, I confessed, Mama? I said, silently tears welled up into my eyes, sadly I said" Mama, I'm sorry"! I blurted out my voice trembled as I spoke, my heart downtrodden I burst into tears, she still looking at me, she asked me questioningly "Why"? I don't know I answered, we were just playing and I went into your room too.

In her quiet way, she shook her head in an acceptance of my reasoning, said nothing more than "um" I want you to go upstairs and clean that mess you made, and when your done, I want you to stay in your room. "Yes mam" I responded, head still low I left her presence walking sheepishly away to the stairwell and went upstairs. This ache seemed more painful than a whipping or any lashes from my family. I loved my grandmother with all my heart.

I wanted nothing more but to please her and make her proud of me, but instead it seems I only bring her pain and disappointment, I wished I could be perfect for her, and make her smile toward me, like she used to when it was just her and I, before all this stuff happened, now it seems like everything has changed and I can't seem to go back to the way it used to be. I picked up all of our toys, straightened up.

I went in and saw the mess we had made and I did my best to clean up and fix it, then went back into our room. I sat there stewing, and brooding about today's event, and promised myself not to steal from my grandmother ever again. Pretty soon it was dinner time, my grandmother called me downstairs to eat, and I ate with them. I wanted to go outside and play and even waited for her to say to me.

"Go on outside with your brother" but what she said was" go on and get ready for bed", yes mam, and went and took my bath, I thought maybe she would burst through the door with switch in hand, but she never did, so I made my way to the bed, I climbed in wondering about tomorrow as I was falling asleep I felt the covers being ripped off me, and the whacking, woke me up immediately.

The twigs met with my flesh across my legs, arms screaming I tried to catch the switches as it came down, but as usual I was too late, I would feel every lash, it felt like intense stinging from a dozen angry bees, I would flicker and jump trying to get out of the way, but with nowhere to turn or run she was indeed giving me the punishment I justly deserved. She yelled "I'm tired do you hear me"!

"Crying feverishly, between sobs "yes mam" I managed to say, all while screaming, the whacks kept coming till she got tired, just as suddenly she appeared, she also vanished. Leaving me still crying, till I fell off to sleep, I woke up the next morning, I looked around for my grandmother, my brother was up already and downstairs quietly watching tv, I went downstairs and walked into the kitchen noticing that nobody was here, but him and I,

While watching tv, we heard a rapping at the screen door I wasn't sure at first, so I sat there, and they knocked again, so I got up and went to the kitchen window opened the curtain and saw a tall fat black man, with a clip board and briefcase in hand. Yes? I answered, The man said yes uh, Is your grandmother home? Sounding very professional no I said, he looked at me with pursed lips simply said.

I know you are not supposed to answer the door, but give her my card, pushing the card through the mail slot. Ok, I said and left the window, and sat back down. When we got hungry I went into the kitchen to put a meal together to hold us least until my grandmother gets home. As we sat there watching tv, my aunt Glory came, and let herself in, all fun and childlike glee drained from my countenance when I laid eyes on her.

"What are you doing?" more of a statement than a question, before I could answer, she abruptly cut me off, "Get on back upstairs, until Mama comes home"! she demanded I silently gotten up off the couch and did as I was told, back upstairs and into my room. It didn't take me long to find something in my room to keep me busy. My aunt Gloria was a medium built, pecan complexion, mouthy type of personality, she also donned a small afro.

Which for the era was the normal hairstyle. It wasn't unusual to find this hairstyle among the African Americans, in fact it was most used as a primary hairstyle donned to signify a movement, or cultural shift, which was indicative of power, independence, an awareness or individuality. But she from a personality perspective wasn't exactly the nicest of all my family members. One could say her heart was in the right place, but somehow things wouldn't turn out how she had hoped, in short things had a tendency to go awry, if she has anything to do with it. With that said, sometimes human intervention could very well turn out to do more harm than good. At some point it was decided between she and my grandmother that she would be the one to oversee my grandmother's house while she was away for whatever reason,

This day I was called back downstairs by her, huh? I answered to question what exactly did she want me to do? Sit down! she commanded, so I took my seat on the living room couch. Silently she sat in her seat against the living room wall, near the phone in case it rings, seemingly waiting for a phone call. Patiently I waited for the next words to come, she was contemplating her wording to me.

I watched her facial expressions, her body posture and overall demeanor. She had strong facial features, lips perfect for her face structure a gold front tooth, perfect straight ivory teeth, which she used to soften the blow of her sharp, cutting bulls eye sarcasm or criticism. Not caring whether whom she is talking to has thick skin or not, required to withstand such fiery darts, that she could shoot off in rapid successions.

She had this air about her that relayed she fiercely loved her mother, and that she will not tolerate any competitors. Anyone that she perceives as a threat, required her to destroy them immediately no questions asked. In my opinion she was always sad, withdrawn perhaps lonely, her facial expression was somewhat readable which allowed me to determine her state of mind, or emotional level or in my case, whether or not she was angry and about to strike.

For the most part she carried her anger in her head, as if there was a storm brewing, and she was getting ready to strike her lightning bolt with direct precision.

Look here, she said "Mama hasn't been feeling well lately and she wants somebody to take care of you, do you want to come and stay with me"? I dropped my eyes to the floor thinking to myself, my mind screaming What? are you crazy?

Not after the way you beat me up and dragged me through the house kicking and screaming! I want no parts of you! I looked up again, it was her turn to watch and study me, waiting for my response, so I kindly shook my head up and down in a yes motion, totally against what I thought and felt inside about her, but I felt like I didn't have much of a choice, the question circling around in my head was, "Where else? am I going to go?"

As if she couldn't wait to let me finish my answer, she said "Good"! her body spoke volumes to me, her body's demeanor said to me, clasping her hands together, "Good"! like a wicked witch laughing loudly," now I can set my evil plan into motion"! Instead she just said to me "now go on back upstairs!" I had gotten up off the couch and headed for the stairs, and into my room. A little while later,

Mama did come home from work or wherever she was, I could hear her and aunt Glory talking downstairs, I couldn't hear word for word exactly, but it was enough information to know that someone else was in the house talking to my aunt. I continued to busy myself with my toys, some time had passed when I heard them calling me, I went downstairs to see what they wanted, and my aunt told me to get dressed,

I went back upstairs and searched for an outfit to put on and shoes, and went back downstairs, and sat back down on the couch I shot a glance at my grandmother, who was sitting at the kitchen table across from my aunt, when we all heard someone honking their horn outside, my aunt said to me in a hurried voice, "come on"! she said a quick word to my grandmother and we left out of the door. My grandmother never said a word,

We did make eye contact as I walked past her out of the door. Aunt Gloria and I walked up to a car, a red Cadillac, I looked around for my brother, but I never did see him. My aunt sat up front, and I opened the back door, the inside had white plush soft leather seats. The driver and my aunt were engaged in conversation when we pulled out into the street, I continued to look around for my little brother,

I knew he would be outside playing somewhere. Pretty soon it would be time for him to go to school too, he is 5 years younger than I. We made a stop, as they left the car, my aunt told me, to stay in the car until they get back, so I sat back in my seat, they were gone for a little while, I had grown kind of bored just sitting there, so I scooted up to get a good view of the driver's seat, and the console.

I saw a radio, near the bottom, one of which had two colorful knobs, I reached for one and pulled and pushed on it, to investigate exactly what it was, when I pushed it, it got stuck, so I moved onto the radio suddenly the knob popped out, when it did I pulled it out to inspect it, when I looked inside I noticed it had glowing red coils inside, I was fascinated and decided to touch it.

I stuck my right index finger inside to see what it felt like, and I immediately regretted it, as it burned me upon contact. It felt like an electric shock to my finger, I snatched my finger out immediately, and jammed the button back into its place in the console, and then proceeded to sit back in my seat brooding over my burnt, singed finger. They came back to the car and nothing was said the whole ride.

I continued to sit back like I had good sense watching everything as we rode by. Eventually I fell asleep, I didn't wake up again until my aunt called my name which jolted me out of my sleep. We piled out of the car in front of a tall building on Bloom St. right off of Greenmount Avenue, it would be the tall building with the painting of a bird on it. We went up the steps, the driver pulled off.

We entered the building and walked up to an old elevator, we walked inside, I had never been on one before so I did not know what to do, or what was expected of me, so I stood real close to my aunt. At one time there used to be an elevator operator but there wasn't one anymore, my aunt slid the door shut then she operated the wheel herself, told me to move away from her while she maneuvered the wheel,

I backed off a tad bit as the whole box we were in jolted and trembled upward. We slowly ascended up to the 4th floor, she opened the door and we walked out into the hallway, walking past other apartments on the right, with a tall handrailing to our left, to keep one from falling to their death on the bottom floor. There was a total of 4 apartments on each floor, my aunt's apartment was at the very end of the hallway that ended the curve.

She had a neighbor directly across the hall from her. Entering inside my aunt's apartment was a short corridor, that led to the dining room it had one window where you had direct vision of the only church on the block. Next to it on the left was the kitchen, that will only fit one person at a time. Coming out of the kitchen across from the dining room was the bathroom, next to the bathroom was an open large sized room.

Next to it was the master bedroom, where there was an adjoining door that connected the two rooms. My room which was the open sized room, I had a twin bed, situated up against the wall on the farthest sided of the room, in front of the 3 windows, my bed was nestled in the natural curve of the building's architecture, my aunt was kind enough to put a partition up in front of my bed, just tall enough, and wide enough to cover me while I was asleep.

Specifically, so that anybody using the bathroom would not or could not see me laying there asleep or otherwise. When we came inside of the apartment, she showed me my room, and then walked out, I laid down and went back to sleep. I woke up the next day, just lying there, my aunt called me and I went to her, accompanying her was that tall fat black man, who was at my grandmother's house that one day.

He formally introduced himself to me, as Mr. Green they told me to take a seat, so I pulled out a chair to take my seat, and everybody locked eyes onto me, Immediately Mr. Green started the conversation off with an air of "I Don't Play!" you can't pull nothing over on me, so don't try it! Which struck me as kind of odd, but I shook my head in acknowledgement of his position, he was a social worker assigned to our family's case.

Ok Jackie, now you are under your aunts roof and care and it is my job to make sure that your placed with family members first, it's my job to call everybody up and exhaust every single possible resource, to ensure that you are in a safe place. He stated that he could have placed me in a group home, "what's that I asked? He broke his train of thought to answer my question, quickly before he forgets,

"Well it's a house or home for wayward kids all basically around your age group, who have no family members that cares about them like you do, some are good kids, some are really delinquent or bad, but all are in the same home together, with very little supervision, guidance, healthcare. Not the ideal place for a young lady like yourself, and if I were you I would take full advantage of your aunt's good graces"

Listen to her, follow her directions, she won't tell you anything wrong, and you should be ok. But I'm telling you right now young lady! In his authoritative voice, If, she ever calls me, and tell me you are not behaving? I will be forced to come get you and take you to one of those places I mentioned earlier. He added" how unfortunate that would be for someone like you" It's my understanding, you have been with everybody already so far, as it is.

Your aunt here, is your last stop! Do you understand? Do I make myself clear? Suddenly I felt a tremendous burden. I just held my head down, trying to hide my really big lips, then sadly looked up at him without saying a word, through tear filled eyes, and shook my head yes. Then continuing looking downward, he and my aunt talked about me to each other, finally he told my aunt to call him, if she needed anything,

Shot me a menacing look then he excused himself, my aunt also stood up, then she walked him to the door, and he left. I sat there numb, when she reappeared she sent me back to my room. I went heading back to my bed, through the empty room, no furniture, blank and completely white. Except the partition which had a few designs and a bed. I laid down thinking to myself, recalling the entire conversation.

Noticing he painted such a grim picture, and how bad it made me feel. Slowly I drifted off to sleep, the next time I woke up I had to go to the bathroom, I walked into the bathroom, as I sat down on the toilet, I looked around to take in the overall look and feel of the room, It was simple, a claw foot tub, with a toilet sink and mirror, paint was all white, with the flooring black and white checkered tile.

I finished and flushed the toilet, peered into the mirror at myself and wondered if there was a cabinet behind it, like at my grandmother's, well look yes it is with a few things in it. I shut the mirror door and walked out, as I left I peeked into my aunt's room, and noticed that she was gone. I continued walking back to my bed, afraid that she may catch me out of my room, only to get really angry with me.

Once there I peered out the window, and from my bed I could see a lot of what was around us. The HESS gas station, big white sign with green letters, across from the gas station was a bus stop, to the left of this building where we lived was a church that basically took up the whole corner, I could see people walking around, but I couldn't talk to them. I figured anything is better than looking at the walls.

CHAPTER 8

I heard my aunt come into the apartment, she would hush her company, so not to disturb me. Talking quietly to her guest, I just continued to lay there, mostly afraid to move, even though I was beginning to get hungry now, in my mind I wondered when would she start cooking? But I stayed quiet and out of her way forcing myself to go to sleep, eventually I found it and drifted off. When I woke up again I went to sit up with my feet on the floor, and I touched something, It startled me, so I sat for a second to let my eyes adjust to the dark, and wake up fully, so I reached down and found a box, upon inspecting it there were doughnuts inside, one by one I devoured them, afterwards I was extremely thirsty, so I went to the kitchen and drank some water, peeked into the refrigerator then hurried back to my bed.

I figured if I didn't make any noise, kept really quiet and stayed out of her way, she would be happy with me. I walked quietly back to my bed and lay there staring into the dark, until I couldn't anymore, and I fell asleep. Another day had come and gone with no food, but I didn't say anything to my aunt. Later that day she called me into her room, to tell me to get ready so that she can take me to school to enroll me.

After that she led the way, with me bringing up the rear into the elevator down to the 1st floor and out of the building we went walking down Eutaw Pl. All of four blocks away, into the school's building Eutaw Marsh-burn Elementary School.

The Principal and my aunt talked, informing her that I did have some schooling, and that I should be in the 3rd or 4th grade by now, and after some testing.

It was determined that I had a 3rd grade academic level of competency. That following Monday I was to start school. My aunt led the way on the way back home, in which she went straight into her room, and went back to bed, and I went to my room too where I stayed quietly out of her way. I lay there wondering about my grandmother, and my little brother Justice, and how were they doing,

I would long for them deeply, in time I slowly began to realize that I may not see them again. It saddened me deeply, I would lay there recalling times I was with them, and what we may or may not be doing together, I recalled the laughter and fun of running through the neighborhood with my friends, the games we would play, chasing each other through each other's houses, marking the street with sidewalk chalk.

Boy's chasing the girls, trying to get a kiss, I even remembered my grandmother being angry with me, because some boy chased me behind the bushes and dry humping on me, my friends ran and told my grandmother who was fit to be tied with me, I kind of wondered if that is why my grandmother didn't want me anymore? Because I was growing up too fast and exposed to life and sex right under her roof.

Sometimes under her very nose, is this her way of punishing me? All these questions circled through my mind as I lay there, all day and night as well. The next day I thought I smelled food cooking, but then I figured maybe it was my imagination simply because I was just extremely, hungry! I heard my aunt moving around between her room and kitchen but I didn't think much about it and continued to lay there.

A little while had passed by when I heard my aunt call me. She sounded far away, so I waited till she called me again, I walked as far as the rooms door frame and peeked into the living room, she asked me was I hungry? As if seeing me for the first time in a long time, smiling I shook my head yes, excitedly, my eyes widened. Before I knew it my feet were moving me into the dining room and sat down at the table.

She prepared me a plate and brought it to me and sat it down in front of me. It smelled delicious!, "mmm" I exclaimed to my aunt Gloria, "what is it" I asked grabbing a spoon, "homemade crab soup" she says, I dug in as if I hadn't eaten in a week, which technically if it weren't for the doughnuts, that's how long had been. She stood back and watched me devour the soup, she offered me another bowl.

Smiling she asked me" are you hungry"? Swallowing the last cheek full, gulp! I shook my head saying yes please! She went into the kitchen and scooped more into my bowl, and came back with more, I downed that one too, highly praising her as I ate, saying "um-mm good! aunt Gloria you sure can cook"!, chunks of vegetables I didn't know your food is this good! Compliment, after compliment I kept going.

Until she had her fill and somehow sensed that I had some motive for such high praise, with much contempt, in her voice she stopped me short," ok, ok, ok"! that's enough!, she warned, "Now your over doing it" I looked at her wide eyed in complete dismay, I couldn't understand why she would be so upset with praise and good words for what she has done for me, for I was very grateful. I just muttered dropping my voice.

But, but again she stopped me, "Look, I said that's enough! Raising her voice, she said "you don't need to overdo it with me! just say a few words and leave it at that"! sensing her anger

I just lowered my head, in failure, with an air of disgust, I clearly heard her say to me "hurry up and get on out of my face!, go on back into your room somewhere!" Suddenly I realized I just made her mad at me.

I was totally confused, and wondering what I did wrong to her? Now she doesn't even want to talk to me anymore, or even look at me! and what's more is that I don't even know what I did to cause it? I felt so defeated, depleted and floored, and I didn't even come to fight, too hungry to fight. My feelings were hurt, and all I could do was cry! Hot tears welled up into my eyes, I could feel the old bay seasoning from the soup.

Started boiling in the pit of my stomach, before I could even explain why I was praising her, she cut me off, and shut me down! leaving me feeling like my thoughts and feelings has no value to her. I silently nodded my head in agreeance, and rose from my seat, taking the walk of shame to my room, I silently heaved, and sniffled obviously upset, all I could think to myself, is that I ruined a chance to encourage her to cook more often.

All I wanted was to be treated like a normal human being, what's more is, now? I really don't know when the next time I will ever eat another meal ever again! The feeling of great disappointment was overwhelming, I cried myself to sleep. The only good thing I could take away from our interaction was the fact that I am full.…. for now. My feelings were crushed. Another day came and after I used the toilet I lay there in my bed.

Sometimes looking out of the window all day at least until my eyeballs had gotten tired. I would entertain myself by using my imagination to describe what people did, and what they could be thinking while they traveled to and from their destinations, I would watch as the truck driver would pull into the gas station with the word HESS on the side. Pull up and park, then get out of his truck walk to the back and unhook the latch on the hose.

Then reach for the latch fixed into the ground and then extend the hose and connect it into the ground hose, then stand there for a few minutes, look at his watch, then remove the hose replace it back on the truck. Close up the hole in the ground and hop back into his truck and pull out and leave. By the time the sun went down, I was so hoping my aunt would cook again, but no she didn't.

She just doesn't know how many times I trembled and shook, feeling jittery or felt dizzy, and forced myself to sleep just so I wouldn't be very cognizant of my bodily functions going through its process for lack of food. Only out of fear of being beaten up again by you! That I refuse to share anything to you about what's going on with me, the many times my stomach ached, and I wanted to come to you and tell you I'm hungry.

But I stayed away hoping you would change your mind about me, and think I'm a good girl and appreciate the fact that I'm staying out of your way, and instead want to interact with me, get to know me, and learn to kindly guide me and teach me about life. Come to learn that I don't need an iron fist nor rod for me to listen. I fear your critical, condemning tone of voice. Because you are so harsh in my eyes I fear another altercation.

More and more I'm noticing I can't seem to avoid, nor dodge your fiery darts that penetrate so deep, and mar my own vision of self, my self-worth, self-value, my self-esteem. Early the next day she called to me to get up and go to school, before I left, she asked me," you do remember how to get there don't you"? I nodded my head and said yes, "ok then go ahead" she finished, I said ok then left, I took the stairs all the way down.

Simply because I didn't want to get stuck in the elevator, that was scary for me, to have her waging her finger in my face because I got stuck in the elevator. I left the building and walked to school. When I arrived, I walked into the office and asked which class to go to, the receptionist walked me to my class, and waved goodbye as she left, I took my seat as the teacher took roll call.

She came to my name I looked at her and raised my hand, she corrected me before moving on, "Please say here or present!" Here! I corrected myself. I sat and observed the teacher as she interacted and I thought to myself, wow! What a distinct difference from my aunt, this lady talks to me, not at me, and she don't even know me! I shrugged the rest of my thoughts about my aunt, the teacher handed out books and we each took turns reading.

Then it was lunch time, we ate and returned to class, I actually was starting to feel better, we finished reading each one taking a turn then she gave out homework. I stockpiled books to take home with me to practice, and to give myself something to do to kill boredom when I wasn't passed out from hunger. The next day I went to the bathroom, I looked peeked into her room, and didn't see her from the bathroom.

I took a closer look and found that she was gone, so I wandered into the kitchen, looking for something to eat. Nothing on the stove, sink had a few dishes, I opened the refrigerator and it was bare, empty, like a ghost town in there. I looked around and saw the trashcan, jittery and trembling I pulled debris aside in search of something edible. I saw a greasy crumbled brown paper bag,

I opened it and saw the remains of a chicken box, a few pieces of French- fries, a few shards of meat was still on the bone, where she merely picked at it, there also was a small bite of biscuit left, I was so overcome with hunger, I shoved the biscuit into my mouth, and continued to clean the meat off the chicken bone, and also ate the few fries that was left. I was so ill, and just couldn't take it anymore.

I had sat on my bed long enough, it was Saturday and there was no school, so I hadn't had lunch. When the chicken was all gone, I was still hungry but at least ok, so I put the trash can back where it was and hurried back to my bed. I heard her when she came in, but I remained quiet and still in my room. The next day I asked my aunt could I go to Church! I could tell from her body language that she wasn't expecting such a request from me.

With indignation she shrugged it off, and said "church"? She asked, "where"? across the street I informed her, she was about to tell me no when she said to me "you don't need to be around all those adults!, you need other kids there too" there is other kids, I interjected, Its Sunday school, it's for kids too. Reluctantly, she okayed it. I left the apartment quickly before she changed her mind.

Headed down the steps for the church across the street, that I had watched from my window for a long time. It was refreshing to be around other kids, although they dressed for Sunday service, I simply had school clothes on corduroy pants, turtleneck sweater. They had snacks sitting on the table, I was able to eat a few, and when it was over I went back across the street to my aunt's apartment building, feeling inspired by the atmosphere.

I climbed the stairs when I arrived inside, my aunt was sitting at the dining room table, the room was dark, except the little light coming in through the only window in the room. She watched me walk in and simply said to me, in her deep voice with an accusatory tone" I saw you at church looking at those little boys! "Don't ask to go again, because the answer will be no! I was completely Shocked," taken aback and thrown for a loop.

I was internally dumfounded and totally didn't see that one coming. In complete confusion, as I walked I wondering to myself, What could she mean by that? Looking at the boys,? Well yeah of course I was looking at them, I observed how people dress, how they act, how different they are from my own family. I was being observant, that's different from being sexual. I would think these thoughts, but never say them out loud, for fear of altercation with her.

Or have her accusing me of being disrespectful, so out of frustration I burst into tears and left from in front of her, thinking to myself, what in the world does she expect me to do? How do you expect me to learn anything? What do you want from me? I felt lost, trapped and confused. I dived onto my bed in utter and complete sorrow, crying bitter tears into my mattress. How dare she cut off my only chance to eat on the weekends? To get away from her for a little while?

Interact with other people, the next day was school, for me it had its challenges, for the most part it was easy, because much really wasn't required of us, outside of come to school daily, do your homework. One assignment in particular was to learn to cursive write our whole name, this request was a new one for me, but somehow I thought it would be easy, and simple but as it turned out.

I was having difficulties and needed her help and had to ask my aunt to help me to learn how to cursive write my name. Boy oh boy it was difficult more than I ever imagined. Initially she admitted she never taught anyone anything, and that I was a first for her. As it turned out during the course of all that I realized I didn't know nearly as much as I pretended that I knew. I think I did that trying to protect my very fragile feelings and emotions.

She seemed to easily bulldoze and trample and railroad at will. She felt she had to break me down mentally to be able to grasp a new concept or overcome a new challenge, by calling me stupid, lazy, stubborn, yelling and screaming at me to pay attention, showing me anger, elbowing me, telling me to pay attention, what's the matter with you? Are you stupid or something? telling me degradingly"

If you didn't eyeball the boys so much maybe you could learn something", You're going to grow up and be a little whore on the path you're on! I cried a lot during that tutoring session with her. Mostly because I was sensitive and couldn't take her gruff demeanor of being critical and downright mean for no reason, it would compel me to tears. It wasn't until the very end that I would eventually, finally get the hang of what she was instructing me to do.

But did it have to take all of that from her, just because I made a few mistakes, or was slow to catch on to her way of teaching me, she would literally snatch the pencil out of my hand, or lose her cool, and say mean things. It was like she had this unrealistic expectation that I am supposed to be perfect and unblemished, and because I was displaying behaviors that didn't meet her expectations I would be deemed a weakling in her eyes.

Thus, bullying me as a result, because I wasn't like her, essentially, with a non-emotional persona. Her perception of me is that I was too cocky in my thinking and acting like I knew everything, and in fact only in the 3rd grade didn't know anything at all. To avoid her verbal assails, whenever she asked if I knew how to do this or that, I would lie and tell her yes I already know how to do this or that.

But eventually she would see that I was lying, and boy she would nail me to the wall for it! Those 3 hours were a torturous nightmare for me, I had deeply regretted asking her to help me. Quite possibly could be the very reason why I lacked the motivation to ask her for anything else after that. I'm thinking I asked for help, and in return received an awful tongue lashing and a verbal assaulting.

It was more than I could handle, plus I was terribly hungry, and thirsty on top of all that! I wanted nothing more than to get away from her, to cry my eyes out and lick my wounds. Although I finally learned to cursive write, I literally hated her guts! After that foray I started bringing my books home, dedicated myself to teaching myself, trying to open my mind a lot more whereas reading was becoming somewhat easier.

Learning to comprehend what I was reading had its challenges. When it came to math, I struggled because some of the concepts had even more challenges, but even with all my determination not to ever ask her help again, I came to the point where I did need help, I couldn't understand why I wasn't doing as well as I thought I should or wanted to be doing, I reluctantly questioned myself, was it true?

That I am stupid just like she said I am? It started out with me daydreaming in class, not paying attention, I also stopped turning in my homework towards the end of the 3rd grade, I actually just passed by the skin of my teeth! The following year in the 4th grade things didn't get any better. The teacher finally decided to do an intervention and have a parent teacher meeting, sent me home with the letter for my aunt to sign but I wouldn't give it to her.

I would take my time going home after school, I would wander through the playground across the street, which was the apartment complex on Eutaw Pl, then over to the supermarket on North Ave. called City Foods, and I would walk up and down the aisle looking at the various items. I would wonder if I had the money, what would I buy? I came to the baby foods isle and slowly walked through eyeballing the label on each jar to find the fruit that I liked and finally chose a peach jar of baby food.

Picked it up from the shelf walked up to the line, noticed it was quite crowded. Very busy and no one was paying attention, so I walked out the door with it, I opened the jar as I walked across the busy street, stopped at a bus stop and sat down and proceeded to drink the elixir. When I finished drinking all that I could, I took my finger and scraped the sides of the jar clean, then dropped the empty jar into the nearest trash can.

Then slowly walked home, went up the steps went into the apartment and straight to my room. The next day I would get up and gotten dressed and headed out to school, midway there I began to toy with the idea of "why should I go to school, If I'm too stupid to learn anything"? I stopped at the playground which was like a stone's throw away from the school, sat my books down on the ground, perched on the swing.

Looking at the buildings began rehearsing what my aunt told me over and over again like a broken record, that dreadful day she was teaching me to cursive write, up until recently I tried to ignore her words, somehow eventually, trying to please and make her happy had slowly died. I became numb inside and that day, I decided not to go to school anymore, what was the point? I reasoned, so daily I would wander around the street.

I sat in different buildings in the hallway on their steps. Then when I had gotten hungry, gotten up and went back to the supermarket, had gotten another jar of baby food, then walked back to the playground again this time I chose the heavy bulky tire swing, stood there pushing it, back and forth, and just when I started daydreaming I froze, and the swing crashed into my wrist bending it awkwardly hard and fast.

"Ouch" I crouched down in extreme pain, picked up my books with my other hand and hurriedly made my way home. Completely unaware of the time, I walked inside visibly in pain, breathing heavily and woke my aunt telling her I hurt myself, she asked me, "what were you doing at the playground this time of day?, why aren't you in school? your supposed to be in school"? Thinking up a quick lie, it happened during recess I told her.

Immediately she called the hospital then took me to the emergency room, we waited our turn, then the doctor looked at my wrist, straightened it, bend it this way and that, finally he decided it wasn't broken, but rather only sprained, he wrapped it, with an ace bandage and gave me Tylenol for pain then sent us home. I was told to stay home the first few days. During which the school called my aunt requesting a parent teacher meeting.

She agreed to attend, but the next couple of days went by with me on pins and needles in anticipation of this outcome. We arrived at the school with my aunt leading the way, we sat down at the table with the teacher, the teacher begins the conversation with how intelligent and smart I am, but also points out a few key areas where I was lacking, this came as an absolute surprise to my aunt that I wasn't doing any homework assignments.

Nor showing up at school, the teacher went on to explain she had sent letters for my aunt to sign, but I hadn't given them to her, she asked me why? I responded with all of my reasonings, I was afraid of her responses to my lack of knowledge to certain things, so I stopped coming to school because I felt stupid or

I think I'm too stupid to learn. I'm hungry all the time because she doesn't cook nor wants to feed me.

I feel stuck in that room and when I try to make friends away from home you make me feel bad about it. The teacher asked me" why do you feel stupid?" I told her that's what my aunt calls me, so now that's what I believe. The teacher was visibly upset and talked directly to my aunt, I was busy crying and so upset, because I had kept it bottled inside for so long, but my aunt sat and sternly denied everything while looking right at me.

Tried to make it look like I had made all these allegations up in my head, and that I have something wrong with me. So, the teacher told her, if this were true what she was saying about me, then she had better get me some help, and quick. And the very next day, she took me to see a psychiatrist at Children's Hospital. On the bus stop to the hospital she asked me directly, "What's wrong with you?"

Where did we go wrong with you? Are you messed up in the head or something? Because if you are we will find out today! I felt bad inside, but then I realized what I said and had been saying is the truth, and no matter what she says to me, is going to change that. The bus ride on the way was pretty quiet, periodically I would look up to see people getting on and off the bus, but when she caught me looking she would tell me not to look at people,

"Turn your head and look the other way!" she demanded in her ugly Cruella voice, just so I would know that she meant business, I did as she said.

CHAPTER 9

I either looked into my lap or out of the bus window the whole ride. We arrived at the hospital and waited our turn, finally they called me inside the doctor's office, and he talked with me for an hour or so.

Then told my aunt, right in front of me that based on her personality and brain function, she would have to make a great deal of wrong or erroneous decisions before she would learn the right way. This is just the way she is hard wired. Then afterward he was talking to my aunt alone. She came out and we quietly headed home, she never said one word to me the whole ride back. From that day a few changes were made.

I started going back to school, and she started cooking a little more often, from hardly never, to once in a blue moon. She also told me, if I wanted to go outside to just let her know, where I am at all times. It was time for the quarter paper to come out, when I had gotten mine I saw that I was missing a whole month and was in imminent danger of failing. I still didn't want my aunt to see that, but, in spite of how I felt, I still gave her my report card and walked away.

She sat upright on the edge of the bed, turned the lamp on to see the marks I had received which were mostly D's and F's, she called me back into her room, I walked in and stood in front of her prepared to explain. With paper in hand she asked me to give account of each negative credit, what is this? and what about that? She would inquire as nasty as she could muster, and why was I absent so many days?

I pleaded my case, but to no avail, she didn't want to hear it, all she kept saying was, "So you've been lying to me all this time? As soon as I responded with "no I didn't!" she reached up and slapped the taste out of my mouth! From the sheer momentum of her slap, my whole face flew to the opposite side in one backward motion, it took a minute for me to regain my composure, as I did so I could feel a raging storm brewing inside of my gut.

I erected myself in her presence, for a split second, then like a bolt of lightning I struck her, with the same exact force that she hit me with! Her face too swung to the other side, just as mine did when she hit me. Then I stood there, and waited, she grabbed her face and looked up at me, in shock, in that very moment in time I could distinctly feel her hesitation, when she spoke, it was slow and deliberate between clenched teeth ordered "Get out of my room"!

I turned my body to leave, but I locked eyes with her as I walked away, I went back to my bed and sat there until my anger subsided, it took a little while after forcing myself to calm down, only then was I able to lay down and find sleep. She said nothing to me for days. A day or two later I went to the bathroom to pee and I saw hair down there between my legs, my immediate thought was to run and tell my aunt, hurry up quick!

That thought was bombarded with negativity about her response towards me, I could vividly see her telling me "It's because your fast!, only fast girls grow hair as early as you! No good man wants a fast girl! I figured why bother? So, I decided not to tell her, that evening I found a hair in my arm pits too!, I kept that to myself as well. Hard as I tried, school still hadn't improved although, I was showing up in class daily.

Doing my homework, as best I could, I still ended up failing the 4th grade. Walking home from school, slowly as I could my stomach knotted up at the sheer thought of handing this bad news to her, and seeing how she would react, and what impact it would have on me. When I finally arrived home, I stood in front of the steps leading up to the building, apprehensive of taking the walk of shame up to the apartment.

Her behaviors toward me, carried a lot of weight, but I was helpless, and felt stuck not knowing what to do, to make things better for us, for me. Slowly I started up the steps, what else left to do but face the music? Step after miserable step until I found myself in front of her door. My aunt knew full well that I was bringing my report card home, unbeknownst to me, she had this elaborate surprise gathering.

Invited our next-door neighbor over, they both were sitting at the dinner table when I finally walked in. I saw a few balloons, music was playing, a little food that she had put together. I was at my lowest, as I sheepishly handed her the report card, I was already feeling like a failure, and really remorseful about all the absent days, and negative marks. She looked at it, then immediately looked at me.

She placed it on the table, then laid it on me heavy! Saying to me," You failed the 4th grade? I had this party all set up for you!, and you show up with a failed report card? If you had passed? We could have had a good time celebrating, I invited Ms. Lela over here to help us have a great time! But how can I? hum? "You failed"! raising her voice now yelling "You failed"! The blood drained from my face.

I was totally and completely embarrassed in front of this other woman who sat quietly looking directly at me, I couldn't think of anything I could say that would make it all better, all

I could do was think to myself, well yeah I did fail didn't I? so it must be true!, It's all my fault, I'm a failure!, Meanwhile just holding my head down, the one and only time I ever saw my aunt get up out of her bed, and put something together for me.

Really nice and fancy, and I totally and completely blew it, the one chance to see her happy with something that I did, something concerning me. Standing there in front of her, she followed up with her final statement, "your punished, 3 days!" no outside, no food, nothing! as I turned to walk away toward my room, sadly I responded ok, all it took was a sniffle from me, and I was bawling my eyes out!

Back to my lonely place, back to me being all alone, back to being sad. No outside? I can't even go to the store to get me something to eat! Inside I was heavy, felt like lead was holding me down with this huge knot in my chest, it was all that I could do, but just cry bitter hot tears of anguish, pain, and intense disappointment at this whole situation. Somewhere deep inside while I stared out the window.

Quietly watching everybody else go about their lives, I began to toy with the idea that maybe she was right, and that anything that she didn't do for me, was because I deserved it, because I am bad, I wished I was perfect like my family expects me to be. My 3 days came and slowly went, I couldn't wait to go outside then to the supermarket. The day brought its joys for some, and pain for others.

The day came when my grandmother fell terribly ill, had been struggling with her blood pressure for quite some time. She and my aunt Glory kept in contact periodically. Up until now my aunt felt the need to share her mother's condition with me. I was in my room happily getting ready to go outside, when in the distance I could hear the phone ring in my aunt's room, I could hear her quietly talking.

It wasn't unusual for me, but something about her tone this particular day was strikingly different and it caught my attention but knowing her I figured it was something she could handle, and didn't concern me, so as I continued to walk out of my room into the dining room headed for the front door, my aunt with her voice raised so I could hear her, said" your grandmother" then her voice trailed off in the distance.

She struggled to get out of bed, to come and talk with me face to face, which stopped me dead in my tracks, to hear what she had to say, as she tried to collect her thoughts and gather her composure, careful not to let me see her falling apart. Repeated herself, I just got the news, "your grandmother is laid up in the hospital, they don't expect her to make it" as soon as the news reached my ears, I was confused as to what was going on, but, but why?

I stammered, meeting her eyes, searching for an answer. The hospital just called and told me" they say her blood pressure is too high, and if they can't get it under control, it will kill her!" We both stood there silently looking at each other, not sure what to do, tears began to swell in my eyes, when suddenly she broke the silence with a sharp bark, "What are you crying for? This is no time for tears, I've got work to do!"

Snapping me out of the trance I was in, I simply walked out the front door and down the steps. Wondering what is blood pressure anyway? Why is my grandmother about to die,? Why my aunt always seemed to rebuff me showing my true feelings or cry? What did she expect me to do with this information? Why my reactions are never right to her? My feelings, my thoughts, nothing about me seems to be accepted as valid to her.

I came away with the idea that she has extreme control issues. If it weren't for the Psychiatrist telling her that it wasn't a good idea to continue down this path of extreme isolation, she would never let me out, outside of school. She would often accuse me of being ungrateful, because I told them about it, little did she know that wasn't the case at all, I was rebelling her mindset toward me, and how she made me feel!

Less than human and more like a caged animal. I reached the bottom landing and headed out the building over to the supermarket, and filled my pockets with candy, cookies, and baby food, then walked back to the playground behind the apartments. It was your typical blacktop, and concrete, broken bottles everywhere of all sizes, shapes, and colors strewn about all over the playground. It was literally unavoidable.

Somehow you learn to ignore it and concentrate more on each other. The only time I could forget about my aunt at least for a little while anyway. It would be nice if the city cleaned up all the playgrounds, by sweeping up all the glass and crumbled beer cans, cigarette butts, hyper dermic needles everywhere. This would help to keep the one place for kids innocent. When I showed up mostly all the kids from school were out,

I would blend right in with them, waiting my turn on the only swing left, some of the other kids sat off to the side engaged in their own conversations, telling exaggerated stories and adding their own spin on things. I would continue to eat my snacks until I felt better. Sometimes it disturbed me that I was a thief, but often times I felt justified, especially since I knew that when my aunt gets hungry she went out to eat.

Leaving me home hungry, and near starvation, she would come back home full, and I would be none the wiser. I learned to survive the best way I knew how, I learned to steal food, just in case she didn't cook, which would be weeks at a time. I would alleviate nightly stomach pains, at least until the next day and I could eat school lunch. I casually walked back home.

When I came inside the house I went straight to the kitchen to get a drink of water, while I filled my cup with water, my aunt appeared talking to me, she says "I have an idea?" I turned my body to face her, listening to her as I gulped my water. Mama "can come stay with us"! She had this look like she had been crying and stewing on this idea all day, with bloodshot eyes looking directly at me, asked me "what do you think?"

With my cup up to my lips gulping the water down, I thought about it, and my aunts lack of cooking and no food to eat here in the apartment, my poor grandmother would die for sure! I lowered the cup, exhaling then as I caught my breath, looked at her and simply said "nope! In that instant her hands were firmly gripped around my throat, wide eyed and repeatedly demanding a response! "What do you mean no!

Shaking me violently as if I were a rag doll, back and forth "What do you mean? Huh? What do you mean my mother can't come and live with me,? Don't you ever tell me no, do you hear me? Do you understand? Then suddenly she released me, then stared at me with rage in her eyes as I managed to get myself together, I stormed off toward my room dazed and confused crying.

School was out and summer had officially begun.

Which meant that I could stay out all day, and come home a little later, which was fine with me, I wanted to stay away from her as much as possible any way, I only came in to either use the bathroom or drink some water. When my aunt heard me come in the front door from outside, she confronted me and informed me that my grandmother was ok now, the hospital had gotten her pressure under control and they sent her home.

My aunt wanted me to go and be with my grandmother for a couple days. I wondered to her how would I get there? She explained that I would be catching the bus, and she continued with her instructions on what to do, what bus, what stop, what apartment building, and what letter apartment. I agreed and she gave me bus fare, and I left. Walked straight to the bus stop and waited.

I looked around and saw our apartment building, and I remembered I saw this bus stop, daily, from my window, never thought I would be standing here one day. In a huge way I was actually very relieved to get away from my aunt for a while, then it dawned on me that she probably wanted some time from me too. The bus arrived and I boarded it, dropped in my thirtyfive cents bus fare, and promptly took my seat, close to the driver.

Told him where I needed to get off the bus, and he agreed that he would let me know when my stop came up. I looked around at everything curiously wondering to myself, why my aunt never wants me to look at people? I looked at as many people as I could, that day especially while my aunt was not there to control what I looked at and nothing bad happened at all. I just blew it off, as my aunt being overly protective.

After all isn't this how people learn, from watching other's, and doing as they do. I arrived at the place where my grandmother now lives, Dundalk MD. I knocked on the number my aunt said, then I opened the door, It came open as I slowly entered inside calling for my grandmother, "mama"? there were no lights on in the apartment, from the rear end of the apartment she responded," I'm in here!"

I continued to walk through following the sound of her voice, I walked through the living room, the kitchen was on my right, kept walking and pass the bathroom and then there is the bedroom straight to the back. She was lying in bed. Everything looked totally different as I looked around, this is definitely not the same house I remembered when I lived with my grandmother, but upon seeing her precious brown-skinned smiling shiny face, Mama!

I ran as fast as I could up to her and fell into her open arms onto her bosom, and squeezed all the life out of her, "mama!" I kept saying over and over again, tears streaming down my face, I held onto her, as if never again in life wanting to let her go! Just kept kissing her with all my might. Up until now I honestly thought I would never see her again, never get the honor of sitting in her presence, to hear her talk.

Listen to her wisdom, feel her hugs, eat her cooking, walk with her, talk with her. To just tell her of the many nights, I sat up wondering about her was useless, to finally have her here in my arms was priceless, absolutely priceless! for me. It seemed like I had been through a lifetime of hardship, trials and tribulations up until now, but as soon as I saw her face, all of that receded, was now meaningless.

Nothing Compares to the overwhelming joy that I would derive from just being right here in her hugs, her love. I would gladly go through it all again if it meant keeping her here with me. She had aged some, even without her teeth, but to me it added a certain level of purity, beauty & grace, that we are not able to find just everywhere on earth. At this point nothing mattered, she was my ancient of days right there next to GOD.

She had a love that resonated with me, that I could revel in, I could definitely identify with it, and nobody else could measure up to it. Happy to see me too, she asked "are you hungry?" Yes mam!, I said with all the gusto I could muster " I sure am"! She chuckled and said, child go on in there and fix yourself something, then planted a kiss on my cheek as she released me, one could tell she missed me too!

I went skipping into the kitchen to forage through her refrigerator, she called out how's school going, aww its ok, It's a struggle though, and math gets harder and harder, I put a ham &cheese sandwich together eating as I walked in, and stood in the doorway of her room, chomping down, she talked while I ate my sandwich, I asked where was Justice, my brother? She sighed wearily and confessed that when she took ill the state came and took him away.

It didn't take me long to figure out that it wasn't her fault for getting sick, it was bound to happen. She was already old when she gained custody of my brother and I, as far as I was concerned she was a champion in my eyes, nothing in this world could make her fall from grace. After all these years had passed it was only natural that she'd gotten older, feeble and sickly.

It would be unrealistic to expect that she would either grow younger or never die. In my heart I knew that she had done all that she could to keep this family together allowing no one to fall by the wayside, if she could help it. She wasn't perfect, but she was perfect to me. She rescued me from my mother who had tried to beat me to death. I loved my grandmother dearly, eventually we fell asleep talking, just like we used to when I was around 5 years old.

The next time I woke up my grandmother was in the bathroom, I lay there in a half state of sleep, half awake, waiting for her to come back to bed, as I lay there I could hear movement in the bathroom, some fumbling around, then suddenly I heard a thud, like something heavy or perhaps someone fell in the tub. I sleepily called out to my grandmother, mama? Are you ok? Yeah she responded, thinking she was ok, I fell back asleep.

I woke up again the following morning she was next to me, under the sheet wide awake talking to me, I had gotten out of bed when I heard my grandmother's sister come into the apartment, she called out, and my grandmother and I both responded, "In here" we looked at each other and laughed. Aunt Virginia had stopped by to clean up the place for my grandmother, and make sure she ate.

I was about to leave when I reached out to touch her hand, I said deeply to her" Mama, I love you!" she said " I know that baby, & I love you too, on her headboard was a scarf, that I thought was really pretty, I asked her where did she get it, she said "ah that old thing? You can have it if you want", I changed my mind and said "nah mama, you keep it" gave her a big hug and kiss and left her laying there looking radiant and beautiful.

A couple of weeks went by and my aunt Glory announced that my grandmother had in fact passed away from blood pressure complications. When she broke the news to me, my aunt couldn't understand why I cried? And how is it that I come to know anything about death, I could never offer an explanation, none that she would understand, but in my heart of heart's some things' you just know!

The day of the funeral, it was so crowded with relatives near and far, we all took turns walking up to the casket to view her one last time, she looked so peaceful. To me she didn't look like she was sick, or that her blood was giving her problems, she looked like she was at home in her bed asleep. I wanted to touch her one last time, but decided against it, I just quietly cried to myself, it was painful to me, to realize we won't be seeing her with our human eye.

She is gone on to be with our Lord, Father God up in Heaven, it was sad to me that I may never get to experience a love like hers again, never in this lifetime that is, something so genuine, rare and pure as a love of your grandparent. I knew this when she lived but I saw more evidence and confirmation when I realize that she would be gone forever in body, and I was left with her offspring.

To me, she seemed more stable in mind, than all the others put together. I felt safer and protected with her than any of my relatives combined, was it she who kept them from ripping me apart? I say this because more, good came than bad, to me while in her care. If she was in pain or any discomfort, she didn't let me see it, nor did she take it out on me in any way. The fact that I would quite possibly never find such a selfless genuine love.

Chapter 10

Like hers ever again in this lifetime was to me a legitimate reason to grieve. Loss leaves you feeling like someone ripped your heart out, smashed it against the wall. When I take a personal self-analysis of what I'm missing in life, the missing piece to my raggedy puzzle, the cork to my bottle, the missing lid to my Tupperware, the stopper to my sink hole, the stride in my walk, the confidence in my laughter, the compass to my journey, the adjective to every positive word you could conjure up. Words like Peaceful, Graceful, impactful, loving, nurturing. Thank you Father GOD, for giving me such a gift, a perfect model of your love here on earth.

That following week later, early in the morning, there was a knock at the door, my aunt had gotten up to answer it, they talked a little at the dining room table, then when they had gotten ready they called for me.

My aunt had taken him at his word and called to report that I was misbehaving, and she was ready for me to leave. Mr. Green had me sit down, and asked me what was going on? My aunt looked at me and spoke up, saying "she stopped going to school, I don't know where she's at, or what she's doing all day, she is not listening to me" It's time for her to go!". Hot tears rolled down my cheeks, as I sat in shock and dismay.

I sat quietly and listened to her make me look like a tyrant. Mr. Green looked at me, and gave me a chance to speak, defend myself, but I wouldn't, I couldn't speak, I was too overcome with emotion, I didn't know where to begin. Mr. Green spoke up and asked me what happened? I sat with my shoulders drooped, my head hung low, just hunched my shoulders, "saying quietly I don't know?"

What could I say that would change her mind? Finally, he had enough, and gave his verdict. I'm taking you to a group home, until we decide what to do next. He stood up and so did I, and we walked out of the apartment door to that old elevator, my aunt shut her door behind us, and we boarded the elevator. He operated the crank and we landed on the first floor, walked to his car, and he drove me to The Baptist Home for Children in Bethesda MD.

We arrived around 9:00am the administration building was just opening up. The buildings looked like cottages, but the feel of it was very reminiscent of an nun's convent to me, the lawn was expertly manicured, trees were perfectly outstretched to heaven, we went inside the building it was smaller inside than the outside would reveal, the office was just off to the right as you opened the door, it was big enough to barely fit two adults, with a large desk.

There was a hallway with 4 offices all together, that gave way to a staircase. I went back outside and sat on the steps while Mr. Green handled my case with the administrator, the steps were wide, with flat sides that allowed you to sit on them if you so choose to. The doors were tall and eloquently shellacked dark brown had two sides with glass that revealed curtains. There were 4 buildings on the whole property,

With manicured grass all around. One building Administrators, the second was for a mixture of boys and girls, the third building just males, and the fourth just females.

Mr. Green introduced me to the lady, and so left me in her care then pulled off in his car. The lady walked me to the classroom where the other kids were, upstairs in the co-ed building. It wasn't quite lunch time yet.

They had what was called snack time, which they served chocolate doughnuts, and fruit. For those who may have missed breakfast, I ate a few doughnuts, and some fruit, and felt well enough and was able to blend in with the other kids. Everybody in class wanted to know my name, soon after we were friends. When lunch time came we went to the basement, which is where I had gotten to meet all of the rest of the kids who lived there.

It was a better environment than was previously depicted. After school, I was given sheets and towels by the housing counselor, and shown my bed, which were set up in a dormitory style six beds to a room. Girls on one floor and boys were housed upstairs, the boys and girls were all mixture, in age and length of stay, which was up to six months. My stay there was short about two months.

Then a worker came to pick me up and she took me to a foster home in west Baltimore, when she dropped me off there were two girls and two little boys, and two older boys which were the foster mother's biological kids. This environment mimicked a home or family type of lifestyle. There were three beds in the girls' rooms, I was pretty quiet and didn't bother anyone, and did what was asked of me also did what was expected of me as well.

They required me to go to school during the day, and after school, we each took turns with the dishes and stacking the dinner table, then after we ate, take up the dishes and wash them and put them away. I was a happy kid for the most part, and loved music I could hear one chord to a song and knew the song straight away, plus I loved to dance, one night I entertained the whole house with my dancing.

The kids all sat on the steps and watched me perform, a song and dance, to a song that was playing on the radio, the foster mom was even impressed with my skills. Afterward everybody got ready for bed, in preparation for school the next day, I had reluctantly gotten up for school, and then came home after school and went straight to my room, I was tired and wanted to take a nap before dinner.

Rather than mess up a good bed, I laid across it, just in case they needed my help in the kitchen. While I slept I heard movement, like somebody come into the room, I thought it was one of the other girls coming in from outside, or school, before I knew it, someone grabbed me from behind covering my mouth, with his other hand pulled down my panties, and raped me while screaming into his hand, then smashed my face into the bed.

Until he was done, he left me crying into the mattress. As soon as I was able to, I gathered myself and went downstairs, when I spotted the front door, I walked straight out and never looked back. It was late November, when I left, a little snow and ice was on the ground, I'd forgotten to put shoes on before I left, but I didn't care I was not staying in that house another day.

A really nice older woman picked me up and took me to the police station, and the worker came there to pick me up, she asked me "what happened? Why did you leave?" I told her that the lady's son raped me, the worker asked me " So? where do you want to go"? I asked why can't I be with my mother? "She coyly admitted, these types of things take time, but for now? she said we are going to need to find you a safe place to stay.

Until we can make the changes you request If you promise not to run away, I promise to do my best to get you home with your mother, deal?" I agreed, the next place I was taken to was to another home for co-ed children in Baltimore County. It was a moderate sized house, upon walking inside of it the office was behind the front door, to the left was day room or sitting area, equipped with a very large tv.

Tables, chairs, toys, game boxes, books, couches, and love seats. Walking through the house was the dining area, with two large tables, that seated up to 4 each, then you can see the huge walk in kitchen, which they hired staff regularly for different duties, a cook would come in and prepare meals for the kids that were housed there, breakfast, lunch & dinner, and then leave a small snack for after 9 o clock cookies, milk, or some fruit.

Then to the left, walking up a few steps you passed the restrooms, one on each side, clearly marked girls, boys, then there were the bedrooms, two rooms one for the boys, and another for the girls, the girls rooms were set up in cot style, three beds per side with a walk way down the aisle, the girls bathroom was separate, consisted of 2 toilet stalls, 2 showers 2 sinks. Across the hall was the boy's bathroom.

Turns out I ended up staying here for a little while, I was twelve years old, at the time living in this house wasn't too bad, they did not hold us hostage at this home, we did have the freedom to come and go as we pleased, I would walk around the neighborhood, when it wasn't too cold outside and hanging out at the nearest playground. The social worker had given my mother the phone number there, and she would call from time to time.

At the front office, and the housing counselor would come find me, to tell me there was a call for me. It was strange talking to her at first, but then my desire to have a family and a real sense of belonging took over, a couple months went by and soon

I was comfortable talking about coming home to my mother, I would inquire about my little brother from time to time, if she has heard from him or not?

She would always tell me no. I would feel kind of sad, thinking he must feel like I do, lonely and burdened with not having a family life. It was dinner time and the whole house was a buzz, had to cut my conversation short with my mother, to get ready for dinner. Wash our hands and take a seat at the table, and we could eat to our fill. One evening I wasn't feeling so well, my stomach was in knot's so I wanted to go lay down for a while after dinner.

I stayed to myself and was kind of a loner personality type any-way, so it really wasn't too big of a deal. I spotted a mirror and laid down curiously looking at myself, and then it struck me to try something new, so I walked to the girl's bathroom and laid down on the floor, held the mirror down and visually examined myself between my legs, for the first time in my life I saw that I had a few hairs on my pubic area, and a vagina!

When I finished viewing my wares, I said to myself, "well! I'm glad to know I'm not a boy" had gotten up off the floor and replaced the mirror, then went to lay back down. A few of the other girls starting trickling into the room, among them was the house counselor, making sure everyone was accounted for and present in the home. In doing so she picked me as the object of her antics, poking fun, everybody thought she was funny except me.

I could feel myself getting angrier by the moment. I asked her nicely, to please not bother me, right now because I don't feel well. She mockingly repeated every word I said, wagging her head from side to side. I saw that I wasn't going to get any peace or quiet so I gotten up off my bed to leave, and go into the other room, she questioned me, "Hey! Just where do you think you're going?"

Walking up to me, in front of everyone, in doing so, she was in my face like a drill sergeant, poking me with her finger, with a sassy tone " Your not leaving until I tell you, do you understand, little girl?" Quietly I backed up from the pressure of her finger, while she was looking down into my face, I could feel the heat from her mouth, and a few sprays of spittle on my top lip, so I pushed her finger to move her out of my face,

She went to push me back, saying "oh! So you think you're tough huh"? then pushed me by the face, forcing my head backward? The last thing I remembered doing is grabbing a fist full of her hair in my hands, and began yanking and pulling her hair, like a cat, I could vaguely hear screaming in the background. Another staff member came running in to break it up.

When they finally pried us two apart, we were both breathing hard, I recall her saying to me "you little (bleep), you yanked out my hair! They stormed out of the room and called the police, then immediately press charges on me for assault, and I was arrested that night, put into handcuffs, escorted to the back of a squad car and driven down to the police station. Waited inside of a locked jail cell for them to book me.

Then afterward I was loaded into the back of the paddy wagon and transported to Montrose, a juvenile detention center. It was a very scary experience to go through. Well of course after all of that, I was very remorseful, and quite sorry that things had to be taken this far. I was sentenced to six months juvenile detention. My mother came to see me, twice while I was there, and in some oddly strange way.

I felt she understood my plight. It was a very lonely place, the buildings were set up like college dormitories and spread out, like a college campus. In our building we were all under sixteen years old, both black and white children were there. For the first 30 day there we were locked in our 2×4 room, behind a steel door, getting served food through the slot, which was only wide enough to receive a tray of food.

The food was not great, but it was better than not eating at all. Once I got through my thirty days there, then they allowed me to walk in a single file line to go and eat our meals at the cafeteria. There we would see all of the many other inmates from other buildings across the campus. Around the fourth of July the officers threw us a party. Everybody sat in a chair in one big circle and talked to one another, played games.

Like duck, duck goose and afterwards, we sat asking the officers personal questions, it was a very appreciative moment for all of us, and we thanked the officers for treating us like human beings. Then of course, we had to go back to our room. There I had my first period, I didn't understand what was happening to me, the guard handed me some sanitary napkins, and told me congratulations you're a woman now!

When my time was up at the juvenile center, the social worker came and picked me up, while she drove, I asked about my little brother, and the worker broke things down for me in bite sized pieces, and told me "Your brother has been adopted by a loving family, which means your mother has lost absolute custody, and all of her parental rights to her son" I sadly asked why couldn't a loving family adopt me too?

She couldn't answer that question, she just shrugged her shoulders, and tried to cheer me up, by giving away her surprise. The worker took me to my mothers' place which was on Durham St. in East Baltimore. She had a two bed-room house right there on the corner of an alley. Only a few blocks away from Johns

Hopkins Hospital, the social worker dropped me off and waved goodbye,

I waved back then disappeared into the house. I felt a sense of pride that finally I am home! That I could exhale and relax, I really was happy to be with her, with no expectations, no presumptions, no pressure, nothing. It seemed like forever already that I didn't have a mother, nor father, my grandmother did her best to alleviate some of that burden, but truth is, I still felt it, deep down inside. My grandmother is dead and gone now, God rest her soul! I still miss her sorely.

I needed and still need a Mother, I finally have my mother here! It's time to focus on the here and now! it's as if time had wiped the slate clean, and we were starting anew. My mother a medium sized, 200lb, light brown skinned, 5'7" tall fleshy woman, born with a cleft pallet, a sort of birth defect called Pierre Robin Syndrome. Back in the thirty's and forty's when she was born, the surgeons were not as advanced.

Like they are now and equipped to handle such deformities, they left a surgical scar on her top right side of her lip, right under her nose, that was rather botched, leaving her with a grotesquely deformed or crooked smile. Due to her condition one side of her front teeth were totally missing, but she had a gold on the one tooth that protruded. She kept her hair in a bush or afro, which she constantly kept dyed a golden copper color.

She had a pie face with oval shaped brown eyes. Coming from the kitchen as I walked from the front door, speaking when she saw me, my man stays here too, so you just stay out the way, respect me in my house, and everything will be fine! Ok? Do you understand? Clearly understanding I nodded in agreement and saying "yes mam!" "Your room's upstairs, if you want to go see?"

Excited I went running upstairs at the top of the steps, it was eerily dark, next to the stairs beside the railing to the steps was the bathroom that you had to walk past, then come to a dark open middle room with full sized bed, then there was my room, in the back with a door, I opened the door, there was light natural light from outside! Inside was another full-sized bed, a tv, a dresser, a closet, and two windows that opened to the street.

Outside was Chester St. & Wolf St. Where all the goings on, happens! My room, the only room in the whole house that looked like it had life, other than that, the house was eerily depressing. I shrugged it off, and thought to myself, oh well, I'm going to make the best of it. A few days went by, and I came in from outside and my mother who was sitting in the living room, looked at me and sternly said to me, in her deep voice.

" Your not going to be staying here, and not go to school, I'm enrolling you tomorrow!" Yes mam I said, clearly getting the point. Sensing something was amiss, I asked if she was ok? she shook her head yes, then I went up to my room. The next day true to her word, took me and enrolled me into Colington Square Elementary School where I faithfully attended ever since. Didn't miss any days, always did my homework.

Sometimes I did it at the dining room table, other times in my room. Some days she would even cook breakfast, scrambled eggs, sausage links, and toast, with a side of hot coffee whenever she felt like it. I would always be pleasantly surprised whenever she cooked, I would give her a kiss on the cheek before I left out for school. A week went by before I began to notice somebody talking at night, I wondered who was she talking to?

I would hear a man say one thing, but the rest was babbling from her. As I sat at the table and brushed my hair, putting it in ponytails. It wasn't until I left for school, that I saw him, it was Mr. Donnie, out of respect I said good morning, then left. Headed off to school like I normally did, I was happy to be home, life was starting to look good, and full of promise. A whole year had passed.

One day after school I told my mother that I was going to sit with my study buddy from school, and work on an assignment for class. I neglected to tell her that it was a boy, a boy that I had a crush on, he invited me to his house, and I took him up on his invitation. I left home and walked across Broadway, to the apartment building that he showed me, on the second floor. I went there and he invited me inside of their quaint little apartment.

He introduced me to his family, his mother and little brother. We sat down at the kitchen table, and I pulled out my notebook, and he pulled out his too, and we began studying the class assignment. I had pulsating hearts in my eyeballs for him but tried to not let it show, his little brother teased me because he knew I liked his brother a lot. His mother announced that she was leaving out for a minute and will be back, then she left.

It was a while before he had gotten up and went and sat in the living room leaving me at the kitchen table, then I went into the living room where he was, and he was laying on the bed, so I laid down beside him, asking him "what was wrong with you"? he responded nothing, and he kissed me, just then his mother walked in the door, soon as she shut the front door she saw us laying there, and asked.

"What are you two doing? In my house!" Clearly frightened, I jumped up, promptly apologized to her, she stood there shocked, I briskly walked past her, into the kitchen, grabbed my books and made a bee line for the front door, and left the apartment! Walking all the way home, kicking myself the whole time for being foolish, for having a crush on the boy, for even going to his house! Now his mother must think the absolute, worst about me!

Boy I had better not tell my mom, she would be so angry with me. I made it home, when I walked in, I spoke to my mother, and Mr. Donnie, and went straight up to my room. A few minutes later before I had gotten relaxed, I heard a knock at the door, wondering to myself, who could that be? My mother answered, I heard a woman's voice talking to my mother, I heard my mother say" oh yeah? She did?

Ok I will handle it, Thank you! And the lady responded" all right, I thought you should know, good night". My mother shut the door. Straight away called me downstairs, "Jackie"! Mam?, I responded as I was coming down the steps, My mother demanded an explanation, "What is this I hear you laid up, with some boy"? "You having sex"? I was caught off guard that she found out. No! mommy I'm not having sex!

That's the truth, I said it with much gusto as I could muster. Mr, Donnie interjected, ok, ok? you heard the girl, she said she's not doing anything wrong, now let it go! Grateful that he understood, I confirmed it, by pleading with her to believe me, that I am not lying about it. When I felt she was ok again, I turned around and went back up to my room, shut my door. I made myself a promise to never get my self -caught up into a compromising position.

Like that ever again. I went to bed. I could hear her and Mr. Donnie talking, she was talking all night long until I fell off to sleep. The next morning when I woke up, I jumped up and got ready, brushed my hair, and ran down-stairs, my mother was up, Good morning mommy I said to her, she looked at me, aren't you late for school? You had better go on get to school, I had forgot my books, and ran back upstairs to get them.

My mother came up the steps and walking straight into my room, said to me" Didn't I tell you to get out of here and go to school? It was something about the way she said it that let me know, that something was definitely wrong! Before I could turn to leave she grabbed me by the throat lifting me up off my feet and slammed me to the wall, my books went flying in every direction. She stood staring at me, watching me as I tried to get back up.

Stunned I called to her, ma? More of a Question to see if she was mentally aware of what she was doing. Mommy? no mommy! What? did I do? The more I protested, the angrier she became, She stared off saying in her twisted grin "you think your grown now? huh? you having sex now? The next thing you know, you're going to want my man! (Bleep?) I see the way he looks at you! With disgust in her voice

CHAPTER 11

Her face was totally distorted, as if she was now possessed! I see the way you be looking at him! If you want him? Well you're just going to have to fight me for him! Get up! WHORE! she screamed, meanwhile quickly grabbing, yanking me by the throat, screaming like a banshee pushing me with her weight we landed on my bed, with her on top of me! At first she just lay there, with all her weight on top of me, I felt crushed.

I'm all but 90lbs soak and wet, the pressure from her weight prevented me from grasping enough oxygen to fill my lungs, no matter how much I tried to wriggle to get free, she wouldn't budge! She said through clenched teeth, I HATE YOU!, I HATE YOU! I WISH YOU WERE NEVER BORN! With that, she bit into my scalp, I could feel her teeth under the pressure of her weight sink into my head,

I yelled, from the pain! I tried my best to scream but all that would make it out of my mouth, was a muffled sound under her weight. The stark reality that she was trying to kill me, or that she just may, definitely entered into my mind at that very moment. Thinking this day I'm about to die! I tried desperately to push her off, of me, while simultaneously inching slowly away.

Well with a mouthful of her teeth dug into my scalp, I wasn't getting very far! After quite a few failed attempts, I would be very exhausted from this fierce struggle, and give up and just lay there, finally I even thought to myself "if I could just act like I'm dead, maybe, just maybe she will get off of me, and buy me some time to run"! I struggled again trying my best to move her off of me, but she herself felt like dead weight on top of me.

After struggling with all my might for a good three minutes, I suddenly quit, held my breath, relaxing my entire body, lay absolutely still and played dead! Or so I thought, I forgot that she could feel my heart beating under her! I just kept struggling and pushing whenever I could, catch a breath and some strength, this went on consistently for a good 40 or 50 minutes or so, until she, herself was ready to move off of me.

When she finally did move, she reached over and grabbed a glass flower vase off the dresser and banged me in the head about three or four times with all her might! I lay there dazed, too tired, too spent from the fight, with this weird ugly look on her face, stood there looking down at me, suddenly I could see that she just had a thought come across her mind, her eyes widened and she turned to leave out of my bedroom and headed down the steps,

I managed to roll myself over to the edge of the bed, were my feet could touch the floor, slowly I erected myself, and stood up, and hurried out as best I could out of the bedroom, blood streaming down my face. She was already coming back up the steps with butcher knife in hand, I saw her face as she turned to look at me even in the half dark from upstairs where I was, half-light from the downstairs kitchen light.

For a split second I saw that it was not my mother! I was backing up as she was now at the top of the landing with the knife, now pointed toward me, I remembered my grandmother, saying" child?! call on HIM Whenever you need him!" I burst into tears, saying Oh my GOD! I screamed, Lord Jesus Please! PLEASE HELP ME! LORD GOD PLEASE, PLEASE, PLEASE HELP ME!

She said slowly taking steps toward me, "There's no god! he can't help you now!" I turned around and ran straight to my room and shut the door, pulled the dresser in front of the door, I ran to the window and threw it up, I poked my head out, and looked around, but I didn't see anybody outside that could help me, meanwhile my mother was at the bedroom door, trying the door knob, pushing against the door to get back into the room.

I could see that the dresser wouldn't hold her for long, because with her weight against the door, it was tipping the dresser? I stood in the room next to the window. Trembling, scared to death, watching the door, thinking to myself? "What am I going to do now"? In that very moment, instantly! I heard a voice, clearly telling me HURRY! get the bedsheets! Tie sheets onto the bed rails and let yourself down!

I looked at the bed, I looked at the door I could see the door was coming open little by little, and time was quickly running out! I couldn't believe for the life of me, that she would hurt her own child! I froze, I couldn't move, scared to jump, because I might break every bone in my body, I just froze! and I stood there and watched my mother force her way into the room with knife in hand!

When she had pried the door open enough, she squeezed her body in between the door and the back of the dresser and she came around it, headed straight toward me, saying," you thought you could get away didn't you"! I screamed, screaming bloody murderous screams and threw my arms up trying to keep her back, grabbing the wrist with the knife, even then still repeatedly she sliced me across my forearm.

Wildly slicing the butcher knife, just shy of slicing my face! I watched my flesh get sliced open, my blood shot all over us, there was blood on the walls, everywhere! I was still calling her, ma! No mommy Stop! No mommy, no please no! Trying to jog her out of the state of mind she was in. But there was no convincing her otherwise! Suddenly there was a slamming of the front door downstairs.

My mother instantly snapped out of it! Stopped, stood still listening, I listened too then screamed out, Mr. Donnie! Mr. Donnie Up here! help! Help, Help me!, Help me! Screaming to the top of my lungs, finally he started up the step demanding to know "what's going on up there"! He turned to look and saw me, with my mother standing there, knife in hand, quickly made his way into the room.

He was able to get a good look at me, standing there bloody. When he walked in, my mother ran over into the corner, by the window with bloody knife still in hand, trying her best, to stand there as innocently as possible, as if she had done nothing wrong, Mr. Donnie walked straight up to her, as he was walking up, He asked her "Hope? What is wrong with you huh? Have you lost your mind?"

Then commenced to punching her in the face, in her head, I saw her head and body jerking from side to side from the impact of each blow from his fist! Like a heavyweight boxer defending his championship belt. He was literally trying to knock her brains loose! From grabbing her face and head did she finally drop the knife. I ran, as fast as I could out of the room, down the stairs and finally out through the front door! I kept running, for dear life, until I ended up inside of a corner liquor store, screaming.

"HELP!, HELP"! "Please, my mother!" before I knew it I had become overwhelmingly dizzy and passed out. When I woke up the ambulance were rushing me into the emergency room, I passed out again, another time when I awakened there was a huge bright light in the ceiling, and I heard a motor going, people talking, and saying "Wow look at that gash! Man! These are some really big dents!, Look at that gash!

While they were shaving my scalp, I thought to myself, "oh boy this must be bad! for them to be saying that!" My left arm was being stitched up, in several places, where I used it as a shield, desperately trying to block her slicing my face with the butcher knife, where it seemed she was aiming so many different times. I just couldn't, no matter how hard I tried to protect my head, my skull. I just lay there quietly and wept.

I could feel my tears running into my ears. My mind kept recalling today's event, images flashed through my mind, back and forth. I remember the thought came that I should have left the house as soon as I woke up, but I didn't move fast enough. I also recalled when I heard the voice telling me to jump out of the window, but I didn't move fast enough. I couldn't help from thinking that this is the first time today.

I had some peace, and somebody was caring for me rather than trying to beat me to death. I loved her, trusted her, and she turns on me, for what? My heart just sank, it ached, my body ached. I couldn't no matter how much I tried to figure out who else am I going to trust if I can't trust my own mother? What's going to happen to me now? I think they shot me with something to help me relax or sleep because I was drifting.

My thoughts which were audible now was fading, to a whisper, then suddenly mute. I woke up, still laid flat on my back looking up into the ceiling, at the bright lights, I could hear a lot of people talking, as I slowly looked around allowing my eyes to adjust from just waking up, still feeling kind of groggy, my eyes locked with somebody it was some lady was looking at me. She had this mixed look like she felt pity for me.

Like she shared my pain and could sense something bad happened to me, then again it was like she wanted to smile and wave at me, almost like she knew me, but didn't know if I would respond back or not. I'm in so much pain still and don't really feel like being friendly right now, I kept looking around and saw other people sitting in their seats, obviously in pain too looking like they didn't feel good, people coming in and out.

Going to and from this direction and that, a woman on the intercom for this doctor and that. Then suddenly out of nowhere, they burst through the doors, I heard a lot of screaming and yelling obscenities, sounding like some crazy person repeatedly telling them" get the — off of me!" violently twisting every which way desperately trying to shake free from them and run, when they were finally in my field of vision.

I could see several police officers escorting a person in handcuffs as they passed by, she looked around and saw me, for an fleeting instant our eyes locked, her eyes widened, and crazed and as if, seeing me for the very first time ever, she immediately started yelling and wailing to me from behind the protective glass, "Baby!, oh my god, my baby! While the officers were forcibly holding onto her. When the realization hit me.

"That's my Mother!" Thinking she was going to break loose and come straight toward me again!, immediately I flinched and my whole body was tense, like a quarter back I braced myself for the impact of more blows being rained down upon me, I shrieked, screaming Mommy No! and quickly turned my head to avoid seeing the blows I would sustain yet again. When none came, I looked around again, this time I didn't see her.

I could still hear a frantic voice fading in the distance down the hallway. They had taken her away, still kicking and screaming, it was all too much to think about now, my head really hurt from the jolting around just now. I lay there trying my best to keep still, the pounding in my head was too much, some lady in a white uniform came over and asked me "are you ok? Are you feeling any pain?"

I nodded yes, behind tear filled eyes, she adjusted my IV, and I was fast asleep again. Later in the recovery room, I woke up and quietly looking around the room, it was fairly dark, but I could still make out what my eyes saw, there was an empty bed beside me, curtains at the window, they were tan, a tv on the wall, the door to the hallway, people were quietly walking about, I also noticed on my bed where I slept.

Were a few brown paper bags, I just figured somebody left me something to eat, so I sat up in bed, and grabbed the first bag I saw, and without even looking plunged my hand inside, grabbing whatever I could, and noticed it was soft, to the touch, but flattened, kind of balled up, fuzzy. I pulled it out to inspect it further, now looking at it closely I could see patches of dried blood, and the most frightening feeling swept through my whole being.

It was hair! I was confused and really couldn't figure out for the life of me, why in the world would anybody put hair inside of a bag, and give it to me? Weirded out and confused I had gotten out of bed to go and find the bathroom, I looked around at everything and as I walked toward a door, I walked past a mirror on the wall, in which at first glance, I didn't recognize who that was, who was that?

I stopped and I took a step back, looked again but this time really close up, and I saw that it was me! My head was shaved! I had ghastly bloodstained cuts in my head, that were stitched up, but it kept bleeding, and drying but has now become coagulated clots. Both my eyes blackened with broken blood vessels in both my eyeballs, my nose was both busted and cut which had a gash that was drying, and coagulating as well, my bottom lip was deeply cut.

Aching and very swollen. To me I totally looked like a little boy with my head completely shaved. Finally, I was able to pry myself away from the mirror and actually go to the bathroom, which was next to the front door. As I urinated, I kept recalling the way I looked to myself, completely different from the little girl that woke up this morning, who had a pretty face, fair complexion, long wavy shoulder length hair.

Compared to who I just saw in the mirror, there simply was absolutely no resemblance of my former self. I was all cut up now, and really sore. I finished using the toilet and went back to the bed and laid down, the nurse came in and told me they were taking me to get a MRI, I quietly looked down as she spoke, she smiled and said to me "you don't know what that is do you hun"?, I slowly shook my head no, and she explained while getting me ready.

The doctors wants to take a look at your brain to make sure there is no bleeding, or swelling going on in there, she went on and on talking about this and that, until after a while I didn't hear her anymore, and I quietly began to stare blankly off into the distance, meanwhile watching the hallway ceiling lights come into view then whisk behind me, one after another, as she pushed my bed, on its wheels through the hall.

Past other people who were headed to their own destinations. We came to the room, and the person who dropped me off, left me in the care of another who would then push my bed inside of a big tunnel like machine, before pushing me through she said, "now?, I am going to need you to remain completely still for me Ok? so we can get the best quality pictures for the doctors all right?"

I nodded my head, as soon as she pushed me through I began thinking to myself, this is going to be easy because I'm going right to sleep. With my eyes closed I could hear the machine whirring loudly as she turned it up, through the slits in my eyes I was able to catch a few of the green lights dancing around, it was like being inside of a refrigerator minus all the food, before long I was asleep when I woke up a little later.

Not sure if it was the next day or what, but there was a woman sitting there watching me, as my vision slowly began to come into view, she spoke to me," Jackie"? I answered hmm? She introduced herself to me "I am Ms. Hutchins and I am with the Department of Family and Child Welfare how are you feeling? Are you ok? I nodded yes, she went on to explain that "the hospital will be releasing you in a few days.

I just wanted you to know that I will come to get you and transport you to a safer place!" While she was still speaking, I shut my eyes for a second, and when I opened them again she was gone! Those few days came and went in a blur, from then on everything else seemed to occur exactly like it, in a blur. She came back and took me to her car, and she drove me to Baptist Home for Children, told me that I would be staying here for a little while.

Until they could straighten some things out. After she signed the necessary paper work, and made everything official, the administrator lady walked me to the dorm and let me go to sleep. When I finally woke up again, I looked around trying to recall what happened, and where I am, I had gotten off the bed and went looking for the bathroom, the dorm room had about 8-10 beds in all.

Next to the dorm room was a sitting room with a tv that sat on the dresser, a sofa and love seat, then adjacent to the sitting room was the girls bathroom, with a wall sized mirror and several sinks, there were 4 stalls with toilets, and a window. I remember standing at the mirror looking at myself, looking at my face and head, which was shaved close to my scalp. In comparison I noticed I didn't look as bad as I did in the hospital.

Which at the time I was pretty shaken up, but now I seemed to slowly be coming around. I used the toilet, then made my way to the sitting area, I sat there wondering how am I going to make friends now? Will they accept me or reject me? How am I going to respond if they do? All of these questions circled around in my head, a few of the girls started to slowly trickle into the room.

All of which were around the same age between twelve and sixteen. We all just merged together, a few asked what happened I told them all about it, and they thought nothing else about it. When it was time for dinner, they invited me and I joined in with everybody else while we all headed down into the basement together where the cafeteria is, and basically forgotten about my looks, and ate dinner.

It was just like your typical junior high school cafeteria, with a lot of loud talking, kids running back and forth between tables. I didn't feel isolated or anything, miraculously I instantly felt a part of the group, and they definitely did not treat me any different just because I didn't have any hair. Later that day the Resident Manager gave me some more clean sheets, towels and pillow case, toothbrush, toothpaste, soap.

Basically, she gave me everything she thought I would need, and afterward she went and found a scarf for my bald head, and told me how pretty it looked on me, all the other kids chimed in and agreed. So daily I wore it until my hair started growing back out. In which it did, a couple months later. The scarf no longer fit my head like it used to. With so many kids together there in that one building, you would think there were a lot of bickering going on.

A lot of fighting too, but believe it or not we all got along well, we didn't fight, no arguments or anything. Honestly it was like we were all one big happy family, looking out for one another. We had the freedom to go anywhere on campus you felt comfortable enough to go, except we were not allowed to go off the campus into the community without the center's approval. There were some intermingling of the residents between the buildings.

For example there was this one individual named Steven, he lived in the long-term boy's building, he would come over to our building just to sit and talk, hang out. We could tell there was something different about him, but we befriended him any way simply because he was a really nice fella. He knew his boundaries that he couldn't come inside of our building, and we were not allowed inside of his.

One day the girls asked me if I wanted to join later tonight, before I could even respond, it was settled. In the middle of the night they shook me and woke me up saying "come on hurry up"! I woke up all sleepy eyed, and followed them, into the stairwell, down to the basement, the boys from upstairs joined us too, all of us kids quietly filed into the cafeteria, some of the kids were already down on the floor huddled.

With their hands extended out in front of them, chanting with a board in front of them, all of the kids were chanting, somebody hunched me with their elbow to chant too, I mumbled something. Hoping to go back to bed. Our building was temporary housing or short term for thirty ninety days, The long term was for two to five years. When my short term was up, I was then sent over to the girl's longterm building.

Where I stayed a few years, inside this building is where we cooked and washed for ourselves, this was new, but I learned to catch on, if I became hungry I would go into the kitchen and put together a sandwich, but most of the time those who could cook well and enjoyed cooking, did all of the cooking daily, we just made sure the kitchen was clean, the kitchen was a community kitchen, as well as the laundry room.

I didn't do a lot of laundry because I didn't have any clothes, so I didn't worry too much about certain things. Every room had two sets of bunk beds in them there were two rooms total, we were basically self-governing and not one house parent was there. I was the youngest in the group, and followed everybody else's lead, if I had any needs that needed to be met I would ask my peers and there never was a problem.

They took care of me like I was the little sister. The time came when I had to leave and go to another home which was RICA, acronym for Regional Institute for Children and Adolescents, the reason I was sent there so that I could start going home to my mother on the weekends. RICA is in Catonsville, MD. which is another type of longterm facility for those with emotional issues, controlling their temper, pyromaniacs, homelessness etc.

It is staffed full time, there is school which is in the basement, and is mandatory for all of the residents no questions asked, locked down facility, which meant that we just couldn't walk out of the facility whenever the need strikes. The plan was to just visit on the weekends, and if things worked out, now that I'm a lot older maybe we would have a better chance at a real mother and daughter relationship.

My mother was diagnosed as Paranoid Schizophrenia, manic depressive disorder, antisocial personality disorder and mandated to take her medications, which were Haldol, Cogentin, Seroquel. It was prearranged that on Friday's I would leave the facility, walk down through Chapel Gate Lane, to the bus stop and catch the 2 buses to go visit my mother. Whom because of her medications was doing a lot better, we were talking a little more now than we ever did in the past.

This weekend It was my turn at feeling depressed and down about my situation, having to live at a group home, being away from my friends, and a lot was weighing heavily on my mind, that I did not share with my mother. Instead I was being sneaky and stole a pill out of two of her bottles and bid my mother a goodbye until next week. I swallowed them while I was walking and stopped at the store and bought a soda and drank the pills down.

<h1 style="text-align:center">Chapter 12</h1>

While on the bus ride back to the group home, I began to feel sickly and weird, then when I finally arrived at the facility, I told the female staff I wasn't feeling well and went straight to my room, before the nights end, my whole left side of my body from my neck down was completely stiff, and stuck, my muscles were locked tight and I couldn't get unstuck! I was mortified, scared to death and panicky! Thinking I was going to be stuck like this forever.

I began crying and praying to GOD to please help me, "Please" don't let me be crippled, deformed like this all my life!" A couple more excruciating hours went by, and slowly but surely by body was returning back to normal, and eventually I was unstuck. I just want to stress that I never again took anybody's medication that didn't belong to me ever again since that event.

A couple months later my mother became pregnant with my little sister. To be totally honest initially I had mixed emotions about her being pregnant, but I never dared disclose how I felt, but the truth was in fact that I wasn't sure if she should parent another child, since my brother and I was taken from her while we were young, how is it she going to get pregnant again?

Give birth to another being when she hasn't even attempted to make amends with the ones she already has? I would go to her apartment and sit with her, see if she needed anything, If I felt comfortable sleeping there I would, if not I wouldn't stay

I would head back to the group home and be there by 9 o clock pm. One evening a staff member asked "Do you walk through Chapel Gate Lane?"

I said yes, his name was Max, and he was employed there for several years now, and I was relatively new there, and he told me one day" I will meet you" I was taken aback but delightfully flattered that he would even take a liking to me, since all the girls including me thought he was a hunk, he was perfectly muscle toned, an ex-football player, turned youth Counselor.

Newly Married at the time, every time the girls and I would see him, we would gush all over. The male staff were never allowed on the female floor, the female staff was not allowed on the boy's floor. The Girls floor was the second floor, and boys were on the first floor, and third floor. We only crossed paths on rare occasions, like recreation, dinner, or school.

He took a liking to me, and told me one day on the basketball court, during recreation, of course it was very subtle, but while he taught me how to shoot basketball hoops from the foul line, he gave me the house number, and invited me there one day. Well that same Friday came, I left the program as scheduled and went walking down that same street, decided to stop by.

I knocked on his door and he opened the door and let me in. I stood inside his townhouse, looking around, at his photos of him with his newlywed wife, I asked where was she? and he told me, "oh, she's at work and won't be back until later tonight" can I get you something to drink?" he invited me to the kitchen offered me a soda, and we chit chatted for a few minutes.

Then he took me by the hand and walked me upstairs, telling me" you know I wanted you? I felt intensely attracted to you since the first time I laid eyes on you!" I told him I liked him too, he sat me down on his bed, and totally, slowly undressed me, kissing me gently and gazing into my eyes the entire time, from there I was whisked away into our secret fantasy world. With the promise as long as I was quiet about it.

We could continue our rendezvous, whenever I felt like it. I washed up and left his place and caught the bus, went to my mother's place, then went back to the program. One weekend I went to my mother's place, she and I had a falling out, and I left there headed to the bus stop and a guy followed me to the bus stop, and wouldn't leave me alone, telling me how pretty I am, how sexy I look tonight and why can't I go with him?

I decided to go with him, and when I did, I had gotten pregnant that night. I kept it quiet as long as I could, but my mother started to notice, and asked me, I admitted that I was, she asked by who? Immediately I felt trapped and was already feeling bad about being pregnant at sixteen that if I told her by some guy I met at the bus stop, I would have made myself look worse, than what I was already feeling inside.

I told her the Counselor Max was my baby daddy. I felt bad as soon as I told her, but it was too late, she had already called the group home and told them what happened! My mother took me to the doctor to find out for sure, and I was indeed, pregnant, the next thing she did was arrange for me to have an abortion, saying You do not need to be having any kids, not now not ever!

Because this would be bad for you! You are too young right now to be a mother, you have your whole life ahead of you. Her words had a finality to it, that made me feel like this was her truth about me, and I believed her. So thereafter I kept getting abortions when I found that I was with child. In my mind she was right. The abortion was a success, but I felt terrible inside.

For my unborn child, for myself and for Max ultimately losing his job. A couple months later in June, my mother gave birth to a beautiful baby girl. I had left the group home and went to Johns Hopkins Hospital to see her and my new baby sister. She, whom also was born with the same cleft pallet as my mother.

A hole in her top lip that went all the way through the gumline to the tonsil, my mother named her Lindsey. In the following months to come my mother made sure her baby had her operation. When I finally went back to see then, she was on the mend, and happy to see me. I felt really close and protective over my little sister, I loved her dearly, we would play for hours upon hours and I would teach her different things.

I could tell she was very eager to learn everything. I also was beginning to feel like my Mother and I was growing closer, and I was getting something I never had with her before, a feeling of unity and family ties. Eventually I moved in with them just so I could be there full time to help out with my baby sister. I slept upstairs near the front door, they slept in the basement closer to the bathroom.

My mother was very concerned about me not finishing school. She advised me to go to job corps and get something she herself had never obtained, an education and a trade. I agreed reluctantly of course, because I didn't want to leave my mother and sister behind, but I went to Potomac Job Corps Center in S.E Washington D.C. When I arrived I was frightened at the first, but I quickly adapted, I was studying for my G.E.D and working on a trade in plastering for the construction industry.

Add to that, I met a guy from Pittsburg P.A, we were good friends, for a long time. I was calling home every couple of days to share what I had learned, and what I wanted to do with my life, she sounded happy for me, I would talk with my little sister. I was happy and I was sure my mother was happy for me too.

But one day my cousin Angela made a special phone call to the administrator.

Who in turn had sent word to me to use the telephone in one of the offices, to call my cousin directly. So that's what I did, not expecting anything I started the conversation off happy, but she broke through and told me " Jackie!" Your mother and sister just DIED! I had fallen totally quiet, waiting for her to crack a joke, and start laughing, but she never did then she repeated herself " They are Dead!!!Its all over the news, right now! They burned up in a house fire!

I dropped the phone and screamed in agony, I was inconsolable on the floor crying, "oh my GOD no! intense pain and agony! Job Corps made sure to send me home to the remainder of my family members to make preparations for the funeral. It was a double closed casket funeral. There wasn't a great deal of people there. Just the other family members. I cried the most intensely at the funeral and thereafter.

I couldn't get it out of my head that my mother and sister was trapped in the basement, when the electrical fire overtook them, my mother was still clutching her baby, at the top landing of the steps. When the fire department broke through the door, they fell over dead, smoke inhalation, then burned to a crisp! After the funeral we went to my other aunts' house, my cousin had cooked a wonderful meal, but I wasn't hungry, so I went to bed early.

I slept in the middle room, which was my cousin son room, on his bunk bed, he slept up on the top bunk I was on the bottom. That night while I slept, I could hear my sister and mother call to me, it was a little faint, like in the distance or fading, but I heard them both calling me at the same time, it was coming from the corner which there was a table with a radio on it, next to it was a closet. But I was sure I heard them through the radio.

I woke up and looked over at it, then gotten a little scared, and tried to go back to sleep, the next morning I told my cousin Angela what I heard coming out of the radio, and she told me" That radio is not plugged in! We just leave it sitting there for decoration, it's been just sitting there for years" I was numb, thinking how in the world was I hearing them call me?

My cousin Angela said to me "maybe they just wanted you to know, that they're ok"? I was baffled. A couple days later I went back to Job Corps. What am I going to do now? I feel so lost, I need guidance, I need a mother, father or somebody? From that moment on I became wayward, and wanton like a freight train out of control and nobody could stop me. I was doing every and anything I was big and bad enough to do.

I was getting drunk while in Job Corps, I was getting high smoking the stuff they call love-boat, which was marijuana laced with embalming fluid. Ultimately I had gotten kicked out of Potomac Job Corps and ended up transferring to Chesapeake Job Corps Center and was wanton there as well. Later I began to somewhat get a handle on what direction I wanted to go in life. I thought I wanted to go to the United States Army.

I buckled down and studied the GED book in preparation for the test, I passed the GED test! I chose the painters trade, and also studied for my drivers' license and had gotten that as well. Then I met a guy named Tony, he was the star basketball player at Job Corps, and he took a liking to me and pursued me, one day he invited me to his room and I took him up on his offer and went and we talked.

Then he invited me into his room, but the only way I could go in was through the window, and sure enough he helped me in, and we made a child together. I Graduated Chesapeake Job Corps Center in June 1988, September I gave birth. I made a promise to stop getting abortions and keep my babies, but my only problem now was that I was homeless. Job Corps helped me to call Catholic Charities.

They helped me to find a room in a lady's house in East Baltimore until I gave birth. After I gave birth at Bon Secours Hospital, I was home two weeks before I had a grand mal seizure from way too much salt, and bacon in my diet. I was forced to make some immediate dietary changes. Omitting salt and bacon altogether. After I took Ill, I called my cousin Angela and asked could we stay with them for a little while.

She agreed, but when I moved in I found I couldn't stay for long, so I moved out. I was driving so I would taxi people who needed transportation and take them where they needed to go, for a price. Which was how I met and became attracted to another fella named "Blue" later I found out he was a drug dealer of crack cocaine, which was perfect for my then landlord.

One night I was with my friend" Blue" we heard a knock at the door, I answered the door, it was a messenger hired by a lawyer, looking for me! I stepped outside to talk with him in confidence, and he informed me that myself and my brother Justice was entitled to a lump sum from the accidental death of my mother Hope! I was shocked, and a couple days later I went to the lawyers' office.

My brother Justice was there too! We hugged each other for a long time, and both taken our checks and left. I went back to where I was staying and literally blew my whole $40,000 on cocaine, cars and crack cocaine! By the time my son's birthday rolled around I was so broke I couldn't afford to buy him a $15,00 birthday cake! The whole neighborhood knew I was a crack head, pregnant and broke.

I ended up moving to the West side of Baltimore to an apartment. I had given birth to a healthy daughter, one day I was out with my kids visiting, we came past a candle and book store, curious so I walked inside to check it out, and found that it was a witchcraft store with all kinds of books on black magic, and white magic. I wasn't fully knowledgeable concerning anything about witchcraft.

Nor which was better black or white. I was looking at the white magic, thinking it wasn't as bad, as black magic. So I chose to buy a white magic incantation book, which was full of spells on various issues in life, if your lacking love, success, money, fortune, etc. I took this book home with me, waited until my kids went to sleep and I went into the bathroom and sat on my toilet and opened the book.

I found an incantation for love, success and fame, and I started reading out loud the words on the page, what I was reading was totally opposite of everything I had saw in the BIBLE, and in the middle of reading it I came across something about a sacrifice, while reading it, suddenly I knew beyond a shadow of doubt that I wasn't alone in that bathroom!

I just couldn't see whatever it was, but I sensed a dark presence, something bad, and definitely didn't have my best interest at heart, I could feel, but not visibly see that something was within mere inches of my face! I was tense, scared, fearful when suddenly I heard my daughter stirring in the next room, jarring me out of my uncertain state, of trying to get more information as to, What exactly was I experiencing,?

What just accompanied me? What's going to happen as a result? My thoughts went directly onto her! That's when I abruptly stopped reading the book altogether, never finishing, and secretly hoped that was the end of all of it. Eventually I moved to Carey St. and ended up selling marijuana, and had dated my landlord's son a few times, I met his son whom was maintenance at the time.

I contracted myself out to my landlord as the turnover person whenever the tenants moved out I would go in and clean his apartments and houses and or paint, also performed minor drywall repairs if needed. Even though it didn't last, we still remained friends. As a gift from his father, whom which was the owner of quite a few houses throughout the city, gave me an old three-story, three-bedroom house.

Around that time I agreed to marry my aunt Gloria's brother in law, after pressuring me for a couple of weeks non-stop, I agreed to marry her African husband's brother, to help him get his green card. I relented and agreed to do so, but with monetary strings attached. I figured since I was helping him to get a green card, I wanted payment in return. This was not a typical marriage.

This was a fixed marriage in my opinion. I attached absolutely zero commitment or emotion to him nor the arrangement that we had. As far as I was concerned this was a business arrangement only. I and the kids moved into the house, I thought to myself finally the pains, and toils of apartment hunting is finally over, we now have a house! Then I started dating a drug dealer, who sold heroin.

Had ample access to multiple bricks of raw heroin, boy I thought to myself, things are sure looking much better now, I was living the good life! I was being introduced to all of his friends. A year later I had developed a terrible addiction to raw heroin, also found out that he was cheating on me with his ex-girlfriend, we broke up. I was alone again making more bad decisions, even had a homo fling, just merely experimenting.

Then I met another man named Scott, he wasn't a drug dealer per-se, but would help to sell it whenever he needed to make a few extra dollars. He too was an addict and liked heroin as well and knew of all the better grade of dope spots to score. (We would search all over the city looking for the best dope in town) We ended up dating. Little did I know I was making GOD angry with every careless, thoughtless decision I ever made.

Slowly I was losing everything, except my addiction for drugs, heroin! I would leave my kids in the house close to eight hours at a time, while I was out chasing drugs. Whenever the next best thing was out, I was among them in the dope lines. I used to bring my kids with me, into the drug infested neighborhoods but the other junkie people looked down on me for doing that, so afraid of the ridicule I started leaving them home alone.

Thinking I was doing the right thing, one day I was in bed napping, my kids were watching tv, eventually fell asleep too and while I slept I saw the outline of a human face, but his mouth never moved, not even once the whole while He was talking to me, but I could clearly hear, words or his thoughts beyond a shadow of doubt. He said a lot but I specifically remember Him saying

"You will look for her, but you will not find her! You will call for her, but she won't hear you! You will search the highways, and byways looking for her! You will check every hedge, but she won't be found by you! I woke up afterward, wanting to shrug it off as a weird dope dream, but I knew it was something else, something more. It was something about that particular dream.

That I couldn't reason away no matter how hard I tried, there was something ominously prophetic about it. A week later I decided to call my daughter's father and asked could he keep her for a little while. To give me some time to get myself into a program or something to help me kick this dope habit. He agreed so I caught a taxi and took my daughter over to his sister's house across town.

On the ride over I was informing my daughter that I would be leaving her at her father's but, she questioned me to no end as to why? Was quite adamant about staying with me, and clearly upset that I was leaving her there, in defiance she angrily folded her arms, and said to me Mommy!" I'm going to die!" and forcibly sat back in her seat, the taxi driver in his rear-mirror shot me a quick look.

Clearly taken aback by this little girl's statement to her mother. I responded by blowing it off, saying "No, your not!, now, don't you go talking like that!, your going to be with your daddy, he's going to protect you, and you will be ok". We were quiet after that, when we arrived I ended up staying for a little while, it was hard for me to leave and she wouldn't let me to leave her.

I eventually went back home soon I began to hear vermin moving around in the walls at night. The next day I went to a program in the neighborhood named Agape House. The administrative lady wasn't very nice, at least that was the impression that I had gotten from her, she was gruff in my opinion, but asked me would I be willing to leave Baltimore and go out of state, I said yes, but couldn't come up with a move date.

Mostly because I still wanted to get high, she sensing I wasn't quite ready yet, agreed to give me more time and directed me to come back when I was ready. Soon as I left her office, I went straight for the dope dealer to get high. I would go back and forth visiting with my little girl, even took my son with me a few times. The longer she stayed with her father's family, the more she wanted to come home.

Even crying making a scene when I was about to leave her again. Ultimately I ended up bringing her back home, but then shortly thereafter she started hiding in the closets, when I asked her why she wouldn't or couldn't tell me why? One day I went looking for her and opened the closet door, and she was just standing there. I asked her why? What's wrong?

She just said she was scared, hearing noises in her room. I blew it off. Then another time I heard crying in the stairwell, on the steps leading up from the living room, on up to the bedrooms on the second landing the stairwells were dark with absolutely no light, to me it sounded like a kid, but it wasn't either one of my children. I let that one go too. When my friend Scott came over I would complain.

To him that I wanted to stop getting high and running the street after drugs, and that I really want to get my act together. He told me" If you are serious I may be able to help you out! I will come by tomorrow. The next day he brought me something, it was a pinkish liquid inside a small white jug, about half full. He told me this will help you kick the dope habit, I asked what is it? He said its methadone!

A buddy of mine is in the program, he goes to the clinic and drinks it, but he doesn't swallow it. The program really doesn't not pay close attention to him so he spits it out into a container and sells it. Don't worry about it, I took care of everything. I was very grateful this man was willing to help me get my act together and start becoming the mother I would like to be to my children.

I took the bottle and put it inside of the refrigerator behind a big pot of food, on a Tuesday. Saying to myself on Friday I will start self-medicating back to good health. Wednesday I had gotten up sent my son to school, but my daughter I told to stay at home so I could do something to her hair for school tomorrow. I watched him cross the street to school, then I went back upstairs.

Told my daughter to stay here until I get back, she said ok, and I left. As I was walking up the street, shortly before I turned the corner, I distinctly heard a voice call out to me, "Hey Jackie! Go Home!" it was sharp, and crisp like a person was standing there, but when I turned around I didn't see anyone, not one soul, I thought that was weird but I just kept walking, and went copped a bag of heroin.

At the time they were naming the dope, the bag I bought was called " balls & knuckles" and then went straight back home, I went into the house and called to my daughter, as I went up the steps.

Chapter 13

She answered then I went into the bathroom and sniffed my pill. Then I came out of the bathroom, and asked her was she ready to eat breakfast? She said yes! Then ran with me downstairs to the kitchen. I opened the refrigerator and I saw the empty jug sitting there in the front of the pot of food, but I remembered that I hid it in the back of the pot, so I asked my daughter who drank this liquid, while holding it up to the light.

I saw there was just a corner left, looking at her I saw that she was fine, she sheepishly admitted that she did, I was a little angry but I calmed her down and told her not to worry about it.

I immediately figured it wouldn't do any harm, since I had never heard of anybody dying from this stuff, so I thought she would be ok. So I continued to cook pancakes and eggs and sausage for us to eat, and we both raced upstairs to get back in front of the tv and share breakfast together.

As we ate she began to get sleepy, I thought it was odd, but I figured it was like children's cough syrup. In which some do make kids get a little sleepy and then let them sleep it off, then they are fine. I laid her down to sleep in my bed, I even lay next to her, thinking to myself when she wakes up I will comb and brush her hair, for school tomorrow. Then I woke up and went downstairs.

My son came in from school and went upstairs into my room where his sister lay sleeping.

He was watching cartoons when he came back downstairs whining because he wanted to wake his sister, but she wouldn't wake up! I told him not to bother her she will wake up when she is ready, I went up -stairs to watch tv until she wakes up, I laid down next to her, and was falling asleep myself.

Told my son to turn the tv off and go on to bed, but he complained and said, "if she get to sleep in your bed why can't I"? I relented and all three of us were in the bed asleep. Somewhere in the middle of the night, I woke up and saw three figures standing at the foot of the bed where we slept, I lay there quietly looking at them, in the middle of them was a container with a bright light shining out of it,

One of them happened to turn around and saw me looking straight at them! Before I could react or speak. He simply waved his hand and sleep fell over me again! I didn't wake up again until the very next morning around six am, I gotten up and went to the bathroom, I came back to wake my kids, my son woke up, rubbing his eyes, but my daughter didn't stir, I walked around the bed to her side, calling her again and I went shake her, but I clearly saw that she was no longer with us!

As I looked at her I could see her veins very transparent through her skin, her eyes were sunken further than normal, I backed up in sheer terror! and told my son I need to get to a phone, I will be right back! Wailing miserably as I ran to the phone booth around the corner, and called 911, I frantically told the operator" my daughter won't wake up!" Something's wrong!

She looks dead, Please! Hurry up! I told them my address, when the ambulance arrived they came into the room, my son and I were holding each other, standing next to my daughter! The attendant saw my baby laying there and he picked her up, I could tell immediately when she didn't move naturally, nor wake up, that she was gone. I wailed in shock, in sheer horror behind him!

As he took her downstairs and put her in the ambulance. When he shut the door, he turned to me and held me squarely by the shoulders, while I was still sobbing and simply said" Miss, I'm sorry but she is gone! She passed sometime between midnight and two am! Then he stepped aside opened the door for me to go inside of the ambulance, to spend a few more minutes with her, when I climbed in!

I sat there looking at my baby, still in the same exact position she fell asleep in, on her side, I wailed so horribly loud, telling her to get up! I read somewhere in the BIBLE once, that Jesus, told Lazarus to "COME FORTH"! and Lazarus got up, walked out of the tomb with burial rags still hanging off of him, and the people marveled! Needless to say, that at my command my daughter did not budge.

When I was done babbling, from the shock of it all. I opened the ambulance door, when I climbed out, and turned around, they pulled off and I helplessly, painfully watched them take my baby away, I fell to my knees, wailing loudly and bitterly in the middle of the street! Moaning and groaning from the intense pain that I felt in my heart, in my gut until there just weren't any more tears left to cry!

I continued to wail anyway it was as if someone had snatched her out of my arms at birth. Shortly thereafter the police were at my house to take me down to the police station to give a formal statement, I had my son stay with my neighbor until I came back. My cousin Angela came over to the house and took my son for me, seems like from then on I was on a suicide mission.

From then on I made up my mind that I am going to die too! I stopped to buy crack and a lot of cocaine, intent to make my heart explode from too much, hoping that I would keel over and die from even the first hit! I put the pipe up to my lips to take a killer hit, just then I heard a knocking, banging downstairs at my door, I put everything down and went to the window and peeked out.

A tall Caucasian man, with a note pad in his hands from the Baltimore Sun was standing on my steps looking up at me, poignant, indignantly requesting that I make a statement as to how my child just died! Watching his demeanor as he spoke, I determined that he had already formed an opinion of me, which colored his attitude in speech toward me. I rebuffed him and his interview.

Later as I watched the news I saw and heard a mixture of great deal of accusations, and mere conjunctures as to what they think happened, in combination of what I told the police under extreme duress in my formal statement. Another week went by mentally inept, totally incapable of doing anything responsibly. Too overcome with grief, too disappointed I wouldn't die.

I couldn't understand why I wasn't successful in killing myself? How was death so easy to come by for everybody else that I loved, but not me! I was a real mess, physically I was nothing but skin and bone, a mere shell of myself even my favorite pair of sweatpants fell clean off my body. Intellectually, nobody was home in my brain, my eyes were open, the only motor skill that worked properly was hand to mouth.

Which was just enough for my crack pipe, there simply was absolutely no way possible that I could make any funeral arrangements, for my own child! She'd just turned 5 yrs. old in February, I was literally too distraught, out of my mind. On the day of the funeral the funeral home was overcrowded with people far and wide from the neighborhood and abroad that heard by any means about what happened.

My friends brought their children and other family members. My daughter's school was also there, the little children were crying as they came up to me and hugged me, I knelt down to hug them all, I wept on their little shoulders. I miss my baby dearly, her infectious joy, playfulness and keen love for everybody was a remarkable quality everyone adored about her. The funeral was over for everybody, they each went home, into separate directions.

Mine? Would never end! I Thank March Funeral Home in Baltimore MD. On Greenmount Ave. for their remarkable service, all of which was done for free on behalf of my daughter. I will never forget their generosity. The Police eventually came back to my house for my arrest which was for second degree murder. Taken me down to the Baltimore City Detention Center, it was all of six months before I had a trial date.

Which allowed me a little time to get somewhat sober before they scheduled me, for a court date. I consulted with Warren Brown, one of Baltimore's Best Defense lawyers of his time. He only wanted $500.00 retainer's fee, unfortunately I couldn't afford it, thus had to settle for a court appointed public defender.

The judge decided that because this is considered a high-profile case, the nature of the crime as well as the circumstances surrounding it. That a few years in women's prison would be sufficient. I was sentenced to ten years all suspended but five, with five years of probation and five years parole. At the Jessup Women's Correctional Center, I was nervous and didn't know what to expect, but then I relaxed as time went on.

I was put in the cell with another woman who was doing time, when I walked in she was reading the BIBLE, and encouraged me to read as well, it wasn't long after we were reading the word, that she took a liking to me and I couldn't put her off for very long. Eventually I relented and we continued to cohabitate for a while until I came to my senses, and wanted out, but she threatened and told me" the only way out is both of us on lock"!

I was afraid to go on lock, (punishment, banished to solitary confinement), because that meant that I wouldn't be able to go home as scheduled, as a punishment this would add more time onto my sentence. So I felt stuck, but then we ended up fighting anyway, due to one of her temper tantrums one night she threatened to beat me up, and was calling my mother and grandmother all kinds of nasty names.

I had reached my boiling point, I actually didn't know I had a boiling point, but she helped me see that I do indeed have one. When she punched me, we ended up fighting like wildcats in that tiny cell. Well needless to say, we both were sent to lock-up that night, went before a hearing a couple days later and was sentenced to ninety days. While in my cell, I began feeling suicidal, and was taken to the doctors across the campus.

Whom then prescribed the medication Zoloft for anti-depression. On lock in a cell alone, I had a lot of time to reflect on myself, and the course of my life. I was faced with a choice, to use this time to either flake out, lose what was left of my mind, or try to figure out what I'm going to do with myself, from this point moving forward. Day after day, it was seeming like the higher power was trying to reach me, to get my attention.

But because I was making all kinds of fooling decisions in the past, out of fear of being alone, low self-esteem, too many men, survivor's guilt, lack of guidance, drug induced hazes, just out of control. I could not, would not hear Him. I cried a lot, knowing that I really screwed things up, screwed up my life royally and I didn't know what to do about it. I remember deeply wishing I knew how to live a good and perfect life like so many others that I knew.

I wished there was a manual or a book that would tell me how to live, how to act.

How to think, what I should and should not be doing for this or that situation, when this comes up? What should I do? Because I keep messing things up! If I have anything to do with it, you can rest assured I will find a way to louse it all up! I felt like everything and everybody I knew and loved something bad ended up happening, and I was feeling like it was because of me.

Was I cursed? Am I doomed for a life of death, doom and destruction? I was desperate and wanted to know why my luck was so bad? Inside my cell, which was a three by six, brick room with concrete floors, a window, a cot and a metal toilet with a sink, a desk and chair. Inside of the desk was a book, more specifically a BIBLE. I tentatively thumbed through the pages.

Then I sat there and just looked at it, after I had cried my eyes out, I thought to myself well what do I have to lose? I have already lost everything, my home, is gone! My children?, well one is now deceased, the other is with my cousin, my life gone, what life? I'm an addict, dual addicted to anything I can get my hands on, what quality of life is that? I'm a mess!

There is something about solitude, and solidarity it has a way of forcing you to get real about some things, about yourself and your life, the direction of your life. Technically my reality is that my life is a bona fide mess. What do I have to lose? I was afraid of giving up all my comforts, trading in my fun, giving up my friends, being generous with my money.

The reality is that all of what I thought I had, amounted to absolutely nothing anyway, rubbish! None of what I thought

I had could compare to what GOD has! I had to get real with myself, I have literally tried everything! except tried GOD! I have depended on other's never once depended on GOD! I literally ran all over the streets, but I never ran to GOD THE Father!

I tried to make it all on my own, strength and my own will, but I never tried to make my way to My Lord My GOD! Everything I touched turned sour, but I never once tried to touch the hem of HIS garment, right then and there I decided to take a chance on GOD! With that I began reading beginning with Genesis first chapter. I knew beyond a shadow of doubt that I needed to get my own relationship with HIM.

Kept on reading, I would read daily morning and night. When I came to the story of Sodom and Gomorrah, learned that GOD abhors homosexuality I was shocked and mortified to find that we are doing or have done a great deal of what makes HIM angry! My mind started calling to memory all of the things I had done, and of course wasn't doing. I was learning some very important things about myself.

That I was prideful, and didn't want to be told, that I was living wrong nor allow anyone to interrupt my wrongdoings, or destructive path. That I was/am a sinner, and living a very flippant, sinful life. A few people from church tried to get me to go, by inviting me to a service, or two but like always, I would tell them, yes but never once showed up, and I would actively avoid them at all cost!

I got down on my knees and began talking to Father GOD in Heaven, and expressed my remorse for my behaviors, up until now! Right then and there I Repented my wanton attitude in heart, and deed! I repented stealing I repented using HIS name in vain, I repented of lying, I repented adultery, I repented homosexuality, (even though I was merely a child, very immature, gullible and experimental. Doing what others wanted, following along. No one never once said to me, old nor young this is wrong and you, nor we should not be doing this!) I repented drug abuse & misuse, I repented unforgiveness, I repented being a murderer! I repented witchcraft, I repented greed, I repented false Idols. When I saw with my own eyes the ten commandments, and all the ones that I have broken.

Compared to the one or two that weren't broken, I knew beyond a shadow of doubt that I was in trouble! Repent meaning to turn away from and not do those wicked things anymore, without reservation in heart, mind. It wasn't until then that I was able to recognize for myself that I was indeed a sinner, my whole entire life I just thought I was living, or merely surviving. The BIBLE at that very moment had in fact became my ruling document.

word for word, in a literal sense. When you don't know anything like myself, at that point, in street terminology very green and unknowledgeable about life, and or a GODLY life? I was easily inclined to reach out to everyone and anyone to help me, guide me, teach me, unknowingly reaching out to the wrong people, people who didn't know GOD, nor cared to know HIM.

When I came upon Moses, and read that he murdered an Egyptian, in defense of his Hebrew brothers, I really didn't grasp the full meaning behind the story at first, Nor did I fully attribute any cognizant awareness that I could make a connection with Moses's story on any level in reference to my own. That GOD fully forgave Moses and used him mightily to carry out his works and ministry, and also shepherd his people.

Whom which went on to become a great nation. There are so many different views one can take, one that GOD fully forgave Moses. Why is it easier for GOD to forgive, than it is for people to forgive one another, or themselves? In fact Father GOD didn't even mention the murder, if I took a comparison of the people who don't allow each other to forget even the slightest error made in the past.

They constantly throw it up in our face, and even belittle us for it, no matter how many years between the offenses. Lord GOD shines through! Another that stood out the most for me was What Great Love that our GOD has for mankind, HIS Creation to perform such wondrous and miraculous acts on the Israelites behalf. He, Father God used Moses was a model, of the relationship that he wants with us, that HE has with HIS Son Jesus.

To illustrate that we as a generation of people need a leader, and without one in place, the people are subject to go astray. I also learned how to say the Lord's Prayer, in which I had much time to learn and practice. My time on lock had come to an end, and I was to go back into population or be housed with everybody else. When I went back into population I continued to read my BIBLE daily, on my bunk.

In order to participate in various activities on the campus we had to put our name on a list, with the correctional guard on duty, and they would systematically unlock our cell, and we would walk up to the building wherever the function was occurring that evening during that particular time slot. Different churches had outreach ministries, that specifically went to the prisons in the community to preach the gospel.

I would also start going to church services, to listen to other preachers give their interpretations of what they read, and how they understood it for themselves. I found it fascinating, how different people can come away with various understandings of the exact same text. When a church came through that was performing Baptisms, I signed up for that as well, in fact I signed up for any and everything I could relating to church.

Simply because I was what they would call, hungry for more knowledge, taking a keen interest in furthering my understanding about the Words of GOD. I also accepted Jesus Christ as my Lord and Savior! I was determined to come away from this experience a changed person. It didn't make sense anymore to not change my old ways.

Old habits and thinking and go back into society doing the exact same things as before. Did that been there already, I learned some very valuable lessons in the process, That no matter how I look at it, I am or was very sinful, with a sinful nature, that being sexual immortality, impurity, and debauchery, idolatry, witchcraft, hatred, discord, jealously, fits of rage, selfish ambition, dissensions, factions, envy, drunkenness, orgies.

Maybe there are other things that maybe you can think of that are not listed here, but those of us who live like this will not inherit the Kingdom of GOD! This explained everything to me, it explained it all. Why was I acting in ways I couldn't understand nor explain away. It was high time that I grew up into a mature adult, it didn't matter where I matured? Just as long as I matured and accept my truth of what I am.

I also recognize that there is absolutely nothing in this world that can take away any of my sin's, nor cleanse me and make me whole again except the precious Blood of The Lamb, Jesus Christ. Luke 15:10. Believe me I have tried everything humanly possible, there is to do to rid myself of this (horrible worldly) blemish, remorse, sins. I found that nothing, absolutely nothing can take it away, not being rich, not being affluent, not being political, presidential.

Not even being ministerial can take away any of my sins. In fact, even if I have never once did anything in life at all, never committed a crime, never broke a law, not even jaywalked in the street, I would still be a sinner in trouble of being cast into the lake of fire and damnation. Why? because the fact is; Every knee shall bow, and Every tongue confess That Jesus is Lord above All each one of us will give an account before GOD!

Romans 14:11-12 if you have not accepted Jesus Christ as your Lord and Savior, you will be cast away! Roman 10:10 If you want to know HIM for yourself! Don't make the mistake of assuming your mega millions, and affluency, family inheritance, or even hard earned riches will save you, because it would be easier for a camel to go through an eye of a needle than it will be for any of the rich to get into Heaven!

Matthew 19:24 Before you look down your nose, or wag your finger at me, or anyone else for being a sinner,? bear in mind whom Jesus said that he came for? He came to do a great deal of work here on earth, among them, truly I tell you, to save sinners like me! like you, like us. Not for those who think they have it all together, and feel they are sinless without spot or wrinkle. Those who suffer with these kinds of thoughts are prideful.

Which is a deadly sin.

Conclusion

Essentially I was released from prison, in so many ways, at last in 2005, I am so very proud to report that I am finally done with the street life, and all the negativity, hardship and spiritual starvation that came with it. I never looked back, in the sense that I went back. I took a chance and trusted GOD, and unlike so many of us humans HE, has never once let me down! When I do look back its with sincere gratitude, that the past is behind me and I'm pressing onward, with precious memories of my daughter forever in my heart. Its funny because now I know what it's meant when I read we are all precious in HIS sight. I stand in agreeance today, Father GOD knows, Now I'm living out the rest of my days in the fruits of the Spirit, in love, joy, peace, patience, kindness, goodness, faithfulness, gentleness, and self-control, against such things there is no law! Those who belong to Christ Jesus have crucified the sinful nature with its passions and desires. Since we live by the Spirit let us keep in step with the Spirit, let us not become conceited provoking and envying one another. Galatians 5:22 I know that someday I will see every one of my loved ones again, and we will rejoice!.. Some day.

Thank You Father GOD, Thank You Jesus for saving a wretch like me!

In keeping with the second commandment, love your neighbors, as you love yourself. I share my full testimony in complete Love.

P.S

Dear Readers,

First I want to personally take this time to formally Thank all of you for reading this book. I'm wondering, what are your thoughts, what would you have done differently if you were in my shoes? Do you blame me for some of the things I did in my lifetime? Do you blame the parents, or relatives? Or were drugs to blame? If you have learned anything from my life's mistakes what would it be? I have reserved a special site for my readers, so If you were inspired or motivated by my story, in any way feel free to reach out and share your thoughts with me, the author, by emailing me directly jrteunekegammal@gmail.com anytime.

Again;
Thank You, May you be blessed
Infinitely

THANKYOU!

Father GOD! For a beautiful son, that any Mother would love to have or wish they had such as the one you gave to me. To my son, whom has disappointed a lot of naysayers! You have turned out to be a better man than anyone ever thought you would be! You have surpassed even some of their own children! The same low percentage of success they had about you? They now have about their own child or children. See how GOD works?

Thank you for all of your moral support when it came to all of my endeavors in life, no matter how hair brained and flimsily thought out they were. Your unfailing love and support is what kept me from wanting to commit suicide when you were yet just a little boy. Even today it still helps to guide my heart and decisions in life. We have each other now, Jasmine would be proud! I am so very proud of you, continue being the man GOD called you be, your life will be as prosperous as you want it!

I Love you now and beyond, Always! mom

www.ingramcontent.com/pod-product-compliance
Lightning Source LLC
Chambersburg PA
CBHW051116050726
47592CB00002B/851